THE AMERICAN WING

at The Metropolitan Museum of Art

THE AMERICAN WING

at The METROPOLITAN MUSEUM OF ART

Marshall B. Davidson
and
Elizabeth Stillinger

HARRISON HOUSE
New York

Bradford D. Kelleher, *Publisher*, The Metropolitan Museum of Art
John P. O'Neill, *Editor in Chief*
Polly Cone, *Project Coordinator*
Elizabeth Stillinger, *Editor*
Roberta Savage, *Designer*
Tammi Colichio and Roberta Savage, *Illustrators*

This 1987 edition is published by Harrison House, distributed by Crown
Publishers, Inc., 225 Park Avenue South, New York, New York 10003,
by arrangement with Alfred A. Knopf, Inc.

Printed and Bound in Italy

Library of Congress Cataloging-in-Publication Data

Metropolitan Museum of Art (New York, N.Y.). American
    Wing.
    The American Wing at the Metropolitan Museum of Art.

    Bibliography: p.
    Includes index.
    1. Art, American.   2. Metropolitan Museum of Art (New
York, N.Y.).   American Wing.   I. Davidson, Marshall B.
II. Stillinger, Elizabeth.   III. Title.
N6505.M44   1987   709′.73′07401471   87-8622
ISBN 0-517-64626-9
h g f e d c b a

Photo Credits

Photographs by Paul Warchol commissioned especially for this book:
Figs. 1–3, 5, 8–12, 14–17, 21, 24, 27–30, 33–36, 39–42, 44, 47, 49, 50, 53,
56–58, 60, 62, 64, 66, 68–71, 73, 76, 78–80, 82–84, 86, 88, 90, 93–96, 98,
99, 101, 102, 104, 105, 107, 110, 122, 123, 125, 126, 128, 130, 136, 139,
140, 143–46, 148, 149, 155, 156, 162, 168, 169, 172, 174, 176, 178–85, 188,
192, 194–96, 201–206, 211, 215–26, 229, 230, 233, 234, 236–39, 241–43,
246, 247, 249, 250, 253–61, 263–66, 268, 269, 275–86, 288–91, 302–304,
310, 313, 319, 320, 322–25, 329, 331, 333, 334, 337, 338, 343, 348–53, 355,
356, 360, 361, 366, 368, 369, 371–73, 376, 378, 380, 381, 384–91, 393, 395,
396, 398–403, 406–10, 412, 418, 421, 427, 430–37, 441–43, 446–48, 479,
482, 485, 488, 489, 499, 502, 507, 511, 518, 523, 524.

Photographs by the Photograph Studio, The Metropolitan Museum of Art: Figs. 4,
18, 19, 23, 25, 26, 31, 32, 38, 44, 46, 51, 52, 55, 59, 63, 65, 72, 75, 85, 89,
92, 97, 100, 103, 106, 108, 109, 111–16, 118, 124, 127, 129, 131–35, 137,
138, 141, 142, 150–54, 157–61, 163–65, 167, 170, 171, 173, 177, 186, 187,
189, 191, 193, 197–200, 207–10, 212–14, 228, 231, 232, 235, 240, 244, 245,
248, 251, 252, 262, 267, 270–74, 287, 292–300, 307–309, 311, 312, 314–18,
321, 326–28, 330, 332, 335, 336, 339–42, 344–47, 354, 357–59, 362–65,
367, 370, 374, 375, 377, 379, 382, 383, 392, 397, 404, 405, 411, 413–17,
419, 420, 422–26, 428, 429, 438–40, 444, 445, 449–78, 480, 481, 484, 486,
487, 490–98, 500, 501, 503–506, 509, 510, 516, 517, 521, 522. *By Jerry L.
Thompson:* Figs. 6, 7, 508, 512–15, 519, 520. *By Richard Cheek:* Figs. 13, 20,
22, 37, 43, 48, 54, 61, 67, 77, 81, 87, 91, 147, 190, 227. *By the Albany Institute
of History and Art:* Fig. 45. *By Cervin Robinson:* Figs. 117, 119–21, 305, 306.
By Helga Studio: Fig. 301.

LIBRARY OF CONGRESS CATALOGING IN PUBLICATION DATA

Metropolitan Museum of Art (New York, N.Y.). American Wing.
    The American Wing at the Metropolitan Museum of Art.

    Bibliography: p.
    Includes index.
    1. Art, American. 2. Metropolitan Museum of Art (New York, N.Y.). Amer-
ican Wing. I. Davidson, Marshall B. II. Stillinger, Elizabeth. III. Title.
N6505.M44   1985   709′.73′07401471   85-7250
ISBN 0-87099-309-7
ISBN 0-87099-424-7 (pbk.)
ISBN 0-394-54847-7 (Knopf)

Contents

Foreword

When they were opened in October 1924, The American Wing's sixteen period rooms, three exhibition galleries, and several alcoves caused a sensation. Here, virtually for the first time, American antiques were presented in an orderly, chronological way. In the period rooms, furniture, silver, paintings, glass, and other objects of more or less the same date were arranged together in spaces whose wood- and plasterwork were also of that date. Until this time, American antiques had most often been shown jumbled among curious, exotic, or historically interesting relics at charity fairs and patriotic celebrations. Under the circumstances, it is easy to see why Americans had not until now understood how their heirlooms related to one another or how they might have fit together in colonial and Federal households. Visitors to the new Wing were absolutely astonished to discover, as well, that the rooms were attractive and inviting. "Colonial America had good taste," exclaimed one headline just after the opening.

From its very beginning, The American Wing has had an enormous effect on American taste. Many people were on the verge of turning their attention from European art to the art of their native land, and The American Wing was the spark that set off the great burst of enthusiasm for American antiques and early houses that characterized the 1920s. World War I was over, Americans were feeling the confidence that accompanied their realization that their country was a world power, and many were primed to appreciate their own past and culture. The American Wing's accomplished and refined picture of home life in colonial and early Federal America showed enthusiasts how to use old houses and antiques together. At the same time, the period rooms greatly influenced the way antiques and department stores and other museums and historic houses across the country arranged their collections. Finally, The Metropolitan Museum of Art, the greatest museum in what was by then the greatest American city, endorsed the artistic validity of American arts and crafts by showing them proudly alongside the arts of antiquity, Europe, and the Near and Far East.

Even though there are today many more American art enthusiasts than there were in the 1920s, The American Wing still focuses Americans' interest on their own artistic heritage. In a survey taken at the Museum shortly after the expanded Wing opened in 1980, a number of visitors mentioned their surprise and pleasure at finding wide-ranging displays of American art: "The American Wing makes an important statement about American art," said one visitor. "For one thing, it says that our art is as good as European art. More important, however, it says that furniture, sculpture, and stained glass are as valued as paintings."

And indeed, it is the melding of art of a great variety of materials and levels of sophistication that has always distinguished The American Wing. It was a concept for which the period room was a perfect beginning and from which the Museum has branched into collecting in many different categories and periods of American art.

The first, and until now the most comprehensive, book about The American Wing was *A Handbook of The American Wing*, by R. T. H. Halsey, who oversaw the installation of the original Wing, and Charles O. Cornelius, his assistant; it was brought out in the fall of 1924. Henry W. Kent, the Museum's distinguished secretary and the man who conceived the idea of an American wing for the Metropolitan, had set forth his ideas about a handbook in a 1923 letter to Halsey. "This book should be written in a popular style, and the old-fashioned, dry-as-dust museum catalogue method forgotten," he advised. Both men must have been pleased by the result, for the *Handbook* sold nine thousand copies in its first year and eventually went through seven editions.

Although the *Handbook* was organized so that visitors could tour the galleries and rooms in sequence, beginning on the third floor with the seventeenth and early eighteenth centuries and descending through the mid-eighteenth century on the second to the late eighteenth and early nineteenth on the first, it remained for many years a foremost treatment both of domestic life in the colonies and of American antiques in general, with special emphasis on furniture.

Other important publications that deal with nearly all aspects of the collection have been brought out in book, pamphlet, catalogue, and other forms from time to time, and many of them are listed in the Selected Bibliography at the back of this volume. Metropolitan Museum *Bulletin* articles have announced additions to and presented research on aspects of the collection, beginning in 1910 with an article on the 886 pieces of furniture the Museum had just acquired from H. Eugene Bolles as the foundation of the American Wing collection. Many of these articles are also listed in the bibliography.

The present volume is different from the foregoing works, for it treats the

Acknowledgments

whole of the expanded American Wing, rather than one of its parts. It is not a guide to the installation, but to the collection itself, and its illustrations have been selected to represent the remarkable range of that collection—from great paintings and sculptures to period-room appointments. Captions provide up-to-date information on each object illustrated, while the text offers the story of the development of the arts in America—not a "dry-as-dust" book, we hope, but one that will prove a worthy successor, sixty-one years later, to the *Handbook*.

John K. Howat
Lawrence A. Fleischman Chairman of the Departments of American Art, The Metropolitan Museum of Art

Many members of the Museum staff have contributed to this book—helping with everything from the correct credit line to tracking down an elusive chair in the storeroom—and we are very grateful to them all. Over the several years during which this work has been in preparation, the staff of The American Wing has been unfailingly helpful, responding generously to requests for advice, information, and photographs. Without their help, this book would not have been so up-to-date nor so rich. Jeanie James in Archives and David Kiehl in the Department of Prints and Photographs have also been extremely helpful. Robert Trent of the Connecticut Historical Society very kindly contributed information and suggestions on the Early Colonial Period. Bill Guthman was supportive at all stages, but especially during research, when he suggested (and lent copies of) source material.

In the beginning, Andrew Solomon and Peggy Kutzen spent summer internships digging out preliminary material for captions and Naomi Godfrey gathered pictures and information. As we were entering the galley stage, Kelley Forsyth capably tied up loose ends. Susie Saunders's hours of picture research and of digging for information in files and catalogues saved the authors months of work, and we extend heartfelt thanks. Paul Warchol spent many hours in a makeshift studio just off the galleries taking splendid photographs specifically for this book.

Besides providing good advice and comfort at crucial moments, Polly Cone, our executive editor, constantly smoothed the way and saw to it that our practical needs were met. Cynthia Clark's thorough and thoughtful copy-

editing and proofreading have benefited both text and captions. Roberta Savage, our gifted designer, has worked with us almost from the beginning, and it is through her efforts that we have been able to present so much information so coherently and attractively.

Elizabeth Stillinger

As the manuscript for this book was in preparation, I profited from the advice very generously given me by numerous staff members of The American Wing. The late Berry Tracy, Morrison Heckscher, Craig Miller, Alice Frelinghuysen, and Frances Safford were particularly helpful, and it is a pleasure to acknowledge my debt to them, one and all.

Marshall B. Davidson

THE COLLECTIONS OF AMERICAN ART in the Metropolitan Museum are the most comprehensive and representative to be found anywhere. Here have been assembled significant objects in every medium and from all periods of American history, including acknowledged masterpieces in each of the many categories—painting, sculpture, prints, drawings, interior and exterior architecture, furniture, and other decorative arts of numerous kinds.

The first acquisitions were made almost immediately after the Museum was founded more than a century ago, and as it grew in size and importance its holdings of American art grew in proportion. To accommodate this ever-increasing wealth of material The American Wing, which had opened with great fanfare in 1924 and enjoyed mounting popularity over the following half century, has recently been substantially enlarged. This new construction, designed by the firm of Kevin Roche John Dinkaloo and Associates, provides for the very first time an area wherein virtually all the arts that have been practiced in America can be coherently displayed, seen in their intimate relationships, and enjoyed in their full variety. The present book is a tour of the collections, and not of the galleries alone. Material that is not on view is sometimes included—and is often accessible to students in nearby storage areas.

The Museum's large selection of outstanding and typical examples provides a fair opportunity to judge the true nature of our rich and distinctive artistic heritage. For a long time it was widely assumed that the early settlers of this country, preoccupied as they were with Puritan principles and with the no less demanding wilderness, were indifferent to beauty. But neither Puritanism nor pioneering blighted the creative side of human nature. Man's urge to create and to fashion works of art was conditioned but not stilled by his experience in the New World; and as the country expanded across a continent of immeasurable resources, that urge was continually stirred by new and challenging visions.

Quite aside from the purely visual attractions of its collections and exhibits, The American Wing presents what is in effect a pageant of our history as a people. It clearly demonstrates the varieties and degrees of skills that were called into play by the changing tastes and fortunes of Americans over the centuries. In doing that it evokes aspects of the past, remote and recent, that can be recalled in no other way, for the arts often speak to us when histories remain dumb. The corollary is equally true, to be sure; we must know history to understand the arts. History and art are closely interwoven strands in the seamless fabric of any culture.

In the pages that follow, examples of American arts and crafts are described, illustrated, and explained in terms of their style, their quality, and their historical interest. The talents of a great many artists and artisans—native and foreign born; some well known, some little known, others unidentified; men and women with varied skills and of different temperaments—are represented by the works discussed. The stories of their individual accomplishments add interesting and colorful sidelights to the story of life in America. That story as seen in the arts is the mirror of ourselves as a people. Year by year our lives and our outlooks are never less than the sum of our past. The better we know and understand this the better we know and understand ourselves.

The Charles Engelhard Court

The ground-floor approach to The American Wing leads from the Museum's main building into a spacious, glass-roofed garden court dedicated to the memory of Charles W. Engelhard. As the visitor enters the courtyard his immediate impression is of space and light and greenery. But stone and marble, bronze, and brilliant colored glass contribute to the atmosphere as well. Here a melange of architecture, fine art, and decorative art is presented as a prelude to the rest of the Wing. This blending of the fine and applied arts is one of the important features of The American Wing, where paintings and furniture have always been displayed together in old rooms. The expanded space provides as well galleries for the chronological display of paintings and sculpture adjacent to similarly arranged galleries of furniture and cases of silver, glass, and ceramics. Until now, the paintings galleries and the decorative-arts displays have not necessarily been neighbors.

Although the courtyard contains only nineteenth- and early twentieth-century arts—giving continuity to the space but not indicating the range of centuries represented inside—it does introduce the diversity of the collections within. From the severe classicism of the 1820s' bank facade through the romanticism of mid-century sculpture to the modernism of stained glass and architectural elements of the early 1900s, the court expresses the character of The American Wing.

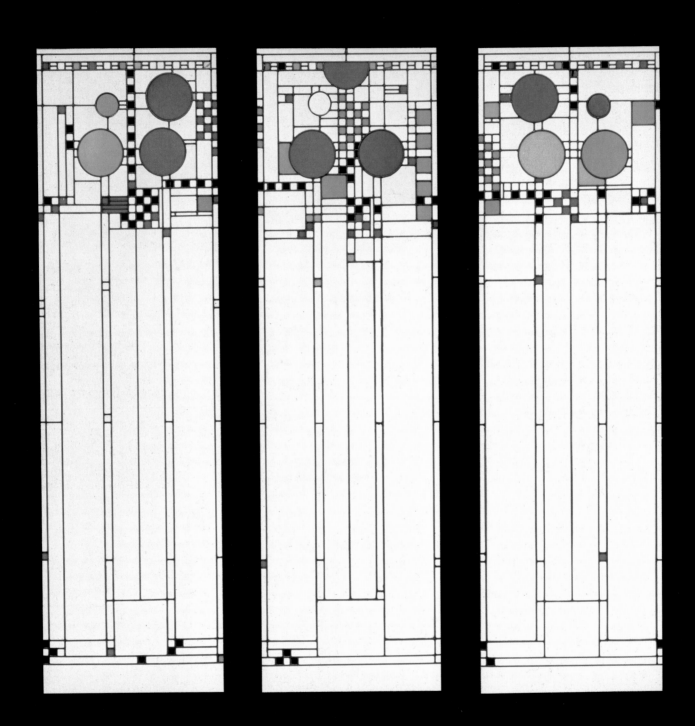

11

Fig. 1. Pulpit and choir rail, *detail, All Angels'*
Church (now demolished), by Karl Bitter (1867–
1915), New York, 1900; limestone, oak.
Rogers Fund, 1978 (L.1983.53.1,2)

Fig. 2. Entrance loggia, *Laurelton Hall, de-*
signed by Louis Comfort Tiffany (1848–1933),
Tiffany Studios, New York, about 1905; lime-
stone, ceramic, glass.
Gift of Jeannette Genius McKean and Hugh Ferguson
McKean, in memory of Charles Hosmer Morse, 1978
(1978.10.1)

Fig. 3. Capital of column of entrance loggia,
Laurelton Hall, detail of Fig. 2.

Fig. 4. Stained-glass triptych window, *Avery*
Coonley playhouse, designed by Frank Lloyd
Wright (1867–1959), Riverside, Illinois, 1912;
leaded glass, height 86¼ inches (219.1 cm.).
Purchase, Edgar J. Kaufmann Foundation and Ed-
ward C. Moore, Jr. Gifts, 1967 (67.231.1–3)

Fig. 5. View of Oyster Bay, *stained-glass wis-*
teria window, Tiffany Studios (1900–38), Wil-
liam Skinner house, 36 East Thirty-ninth Street,
New York, about 1905; leaded glass, 72¾ by
66½ inches (184.8 by 168.9 cm.).
From the McKean Collection through the courtesy of
the Morse Gallery of Art, Winter Park, Florida

Fig. 6. Diana, *by Augustus Saint-Gaudens*
(1848–1907), 1891, this cast 1928; gilded
bronze, height 112 inches (284.5 cm.).
Rogers Fund, 1928 (28.101)

Fig. 7. Struggle of the Two Natures in Man, *by*
George Grey Barnard (1863–1938), 1894;
marble, height 101½ inches (257.8 cm.).
Gift of Alfred Corning Clark, 1896 (96.11)

Figs. 8, 9, and 10. Staircase *(one of a pair)*
and details, Chicago Stock Exchange Building,
designed by Louis H. Sullivan (1856–1924),
1893; cast iron with electroplated copper finish,
mahogany.
Purchase, Mr. and Mrs. James Biddle Gift and Emily
C. Chadbourne Bequest, 1972 (1972.50.1–4)

Fig. 11. Trumpeting angel, *detail, pulpit and*
choir rail, All Angels' Church (now demolished),
by Karl Bitter (1867–1915), New York, 1900;
oak.
Lent by All Angel's Church, 1978 (L.1983.53.1,2)

New Englanders so largely did, and the houses they built in the New World took different forms that expressed their varied inheritances. There is no such thing as a standard seventeenth-century southern house.

Brick—and stone—were also used in New England, but wood was by far the favored building material. Contrary to the persistent legend that the earliest colonists built their own homes, trained carpenters built even the simplest houses in the Massachusetts Bay Colony. Most of them were young men who had completed their apprenticeship in England under master workmen skilled in traditional building practices. Almost 150 of these trained craftsmen are known to have arrived in Massachusetts before the middle of the seventeenth century. Even so, there was a shortage of skilled labor to meet the building boom of those days. This should be no cause for surprise, since during what is known as the Great Migration alone (roughly, the decade between 1630 and 1640) probably as many as twenty thousand discontented Englishmen left their homes to start life afresh in New England.

The typical framed houses that replaced improvised primitive shelters were made of stout oak timbers securely united by mortise and tenon joints. Raising a house frame about an ample chimney pile was a communal effort and was accompanied by spirited ceremony and ample potables. In both construction and design these dwellings were all but identical with English models. There was no such thing as a professional architect in the earliest colonial years; the very word "architect" was not in the common provincial vocabulary. Immigrant carpenters came equipped with neither plans, cross sections, scale models, nor pattern books. Without consciously striving to achieve a "style," but using traditional structural techniques that had been passed down from one generation to another, they built houses that served practical domestic needs according to the accepted standards of the day. For the most part, the individual elements used for construction were cut and hewn where it was most convenient for the carpenters, and the frames were then transported to the building site. Each piece was carefully incised with Roman numerals (which often can still be seen in early houses) to indicate its proper place when the frame was assembled and raised. In a sense these structures were early examples of prefabricated houses. (There were no log cabins built in the first English colonies in America. These were introduced by the Swedes who settled along the Delaware River in the late 1630s.)

Scattered about the New England countryside are several dozen seventeenth-century structures that have withstood most of the hazards to which such buildings have been subjected for

more than three centuries—fire, neglect, hurricanes, and wreckers' tools. Their number is diminishing, and few that have survived have escaped alteration. From time to time changes and additions—lean-tos and ells—were made until sometimes, as in the case of the House of the Seven Gables in Salem, the result is a picturesque agglomeration of different elements. On the other hand, some of these old structures have been carefully restored to their earliest state and others that had completely disappeared have been meticulously reconstructed. Enough evidence remains for us to recognize their essential character—foursquare floor plans; steep pitched roofs crowned by chimneys rising like capstones above the shingles; clapboard exterior walls pierced by small casement windows; and, often, overhanging upper stories with decorative pendents and knobs to add interest.

There were more than a few buildings, both private and public, that were much larger and more elaborate than any that have survived. It was reported in 1676 that among some 1,500 families in Boston there were fifteen merchants worth about £50,000 each—dramatic evidence of the flourishing trade that had already developed in and out of that little port. Theophilus Eaton, a well-to-do London merchant, came to Boston in 1637, moved to New Haven the next year, and became the first governor of that fledgling colony. There he soon built what must have been one of the most pretentious houses of the time. It was a U-shaped structure with a great central hall flanked by two gabled ells, and it had at least ten rooms and five chimneys. Old College at Harvard, constructed in 1642, was another extremely impressive pile; and there were other buildings scattered about the colonies that were of hardly less imposing size and interest. However, it is one of the sad accidents of American history that these have all disappeared, leaving few remaining traces.

In passing, the 1657 inventory of Eaton's New Haven establishment includes a startling variety of what would at the time have been considered luxurious accessories. Among these were clocks; glassware; tapestries, Turkey work and various other textiles; silver; and over 250 pounds of pewter utensils. This is of particular interest since at about this same time the English diarist Samuel Pepys complained that at a formal dinner in London he was obliged to eat from wooden trenchers and drink from earthenware pitchers.

One exceptional building that remains standing to testify to the ambitious architectural works of the early New England builders is the First Parish Church, also known as the Old Ship Meetinghouse, at Hingham, Massachusetts, erected in 1681 and still serving its community. The openly revealed timber framework of this venerable example is typical of seventeenth-century furniture as well as architecture. The heavy roughhewn trusses constructed above the large central gallery on the third floor of the Wing are adapted from those at Hingham, and the space serves as a sympathetic setting for the foursquare oaken chests, cupboards, tables, and stools of the seventeenth century.

Hart Room

*Fig. 13. **Hart Room**, Ipswich, Massachusetts, before 1674. Edward Johnson was able to write of New England by 1642, "the Lord hath been pleased to turn all the wigwams, huts and hovels the English dwelt in at their first coming, into orderly, fair and well built houses, well furnished many of them." Fair and well-built Thomas Hart's house certainly was, and because its architectural framework is visible, as it was in all seventeenth-century New England buildings, the strength and solidity of each post and beam are revealed. The same molding planes that softened the sharp edges of the summer beam and the boards on the fireplace wall also shaped parts of cupboards, chests, and other wooden objects. Walls are whitewashed, the floor is bare, and comfort is at a minimum. Thomas Hart, the first owner of this room, was a tanner. He lived modestly and would not have had the number of sophisticated joined pieces seen here. Rather, the Hart Room has been used to give an idea of what kinds of objects were available in seventeenth-century New England and to bring together a group of furnishings that were made at about the same time the house was built. The ample cushions on the Carver chair and joint stool and the cupboard cloth, all of red wool fabric, show that although the lines of seventeenth-century furniture were uncompromising, cushions and cloths softened hard seats and added color to interiors. Using the top of the court cupboard—which was, with the press cupboard, the most important fur-*

13

The earliest of the Museum's American rooms, from the Thomas Hart
house, built in Ipswich, Massachusetts,
before 1674, shares the central gallery's
forthright architectural appeal (Fig.
13). Its massive fireplace lined with
large, irregular bricks suggests the size
of the central chimney pile about which
the house was constructed. Hand-hewn
oak corner posts, horizontal supports,
or girts, and the huge chamfered summer beam that spans the room from the
chimney to the end wall of the house
and acts as a major framing unit, all securely joined by mortises and tenons,
frankly reveal the structural skeleton of
the building. Clay and sun-dried brick,
now visible in one exposed section, were
used to fill the walls between the studs.
White plaster conceals this filling on
three walls, and boards lightly molded
at the joins sheathe the fireplace wall. In
1632 Thomas Dudley improved the
walls of his house with similar vertical
sheathing and was thereupon called to
account for his extravagance by John
Winthrop, first governor of the Massachusetts Bay Colony. "His answer now
was," reported the governor, "that it was
for the warmth of his house, and the
charge was little, being but clapboards
nailed to the wall in the form of wainscot."

Wrought-iron hinges of various designs support the boarded doors of the
room. The small casement windows
with their diamond-shaped leaded
panes are facsimiles of the originals.
Houses of this period were poorly
heated and inadequately ventilated;
their large fireplaces sucked in copious
drafts of cold air. Benjamin Franklin
once remarked that, seated close to a
roaring fire of a winter night, one
scorched before and froze behind.

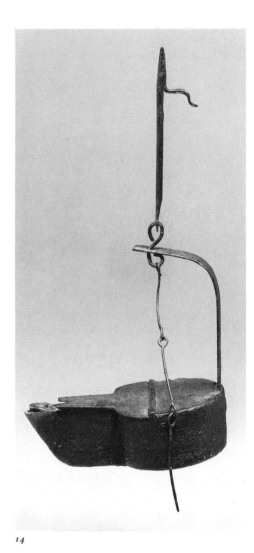

14

Fig. 14. Betty lamp, *American, eighteenth or
nineteenth century; iron, height 10 inches (25.4
cm.). Betty lamps, which burn fat or oil from a
variety of animals and fish, have a history that
goes back at least as far as Roman times. They
work very simply: a wick soaked in fat protrudes
from the slanted spout and, when lit, gives off a
dim light. The handle that curves up and over
the betty is attached to a combination hook and
spike, so that the lamp could either be hung on a
piece of furniture or stuck into the wall or fireplace. Although this example is later than most of
the other objects in the room, it represents similar
lamps of earlier periods.*
Gift of Mrs. Russell Sage, 1909 (10.125.638)

15

16

There was little hope of warming the room throughout, and none at all of heating the whole house. The feeble glow of open grease or oil lamps (Fig. 14), candles of dubious quality, and rushlights was the only supplement to firelight. Nor did the small casement windows admit much light, for glass was costly and of poor quality. A truly satisfactory lamp was not contrived until the late eighteenth century, and earlier devices smelled more or less disagreeable according to the nature of the illuminant, be it animal fat, homemade tallow, or a similar substance.

This was the principal room of the Hart house, known as the hall, in which domestic life centered. It was a living area that recalled in its various functions the all-purpose "great hall" of early English manors. In such rooms most of the vital activity of the house took place, especially in winter when other rooms were closed off to conserve heat. Here the cooking was done (before separate kitchens were added) and here the family often ate, sometimes slept, and usually stored a miscellany of household and other gear that might have included anything from firearms to farming equipment. At a time when, as in Plymouth and other seventeenth-century communities, the average household consisted of nine or ten persons, the congestion can hardly be imagined. The Museum's installation therefore incorporates the types of objects that might have been used in such a room, but it does not attempt to simulate the flavor of life as it was lived by the Hart family in the seventeenth century—an impossible task at the distance of nearly three hundred years.

However, the varied character of the furnishings of the Hart Room does reflect the different uses to which this small area was put. The recessed bake oven and the cooking utensils at the fireplace speak for themselves. Most of the oak and pine furniture, such as the court cupboard and drop-leaf table, is of Massachusetts origin. The Hart Room also contains an oak chair whose back can be lowered to rest on the arms and serve as a tabletop (Fig. 17); this represents another space-saving form, one that was mentioned in Massachusetts inventories as early as 1644. And a rocking cradle (Fig. 15) stands beside the low bedstead that occupies the corner opposite the fireplace. Thomas Hart's inventory indicates that originally this room contained the best bed, a high-post example with curtains. Almost no seventeenth-century American bedsteads have survived, however, and this low-post bed of somewhat later date simply reminds one that every room of most seventeenth-century houses was used for sleeping as well as for many other things. It was probably in such a room that, in the winter of 1631, the aforesaid Thomas Dudley, trying to write by the light of the fire, explained that his whole family had congregated to keep warm, "though they break good manners, and make mee many times forget what I would say, and say what I would not."

Fig. 17. Hart Room, *detail. Chest, Massachusetts, Ipswich area, 1660–1700; oak, 28½ by 41½ inches (72.4 by 105.4 cm.). Chair-table, New England, 1675–1700; oak, pine, height of seat 19½ inches (49.5 cm.). One of a group of carved chests that are attributed to the school of joinery established in Ipswich by William Searle and Thomas Dennis, this chest is covered with low-relief carving. Its ornamental motifs, including stylized S-scrolls, leaves, flowers, and lozenges (diamond shapes), are characteristic of the Searle-Dennis vocabulary, which these men brought with them from their native Devonshire, England. Like the chest, the now rare chair-table is of framed construction. The shape of its original top is not known, for this is a replacement.*

This form was made to perform the tasks of a table when the hinged top was down and of a chair when the top was swiveled up.
Gift of Mrs. Russell Sage, 1909 (10.125.24), and Gift of Mrs. Russell Sage, 1909 (10.125.697)

17

Wentworth Room

Fig. 19. House built by John Wentworth *of Portsmouth, New Hampshire, in 1695–1700. When the Museum bought it in 1926, the dwelling had been removed from this site on the grassy banks of Puddle Dock Creek and was sitting in a dump, "a grisly wraith of its former self." The Museum's Wentworth Stair was located just inside the front door; the Wentworth Room was on the second floor, above and to the right of the front door.*
From *The Homes of Our Ancestors*, by Edwin Whitefield, 1886. Photograph courtesy of The New-York Historical Society

18

Fig. 18. **Lieutenant Governor John Wentworth** *(1671–1730), by Joseph Blackburn (active in America 1754–63), 1760; oil on canvas, 92 by 57¼ inches (233.7 by 145.4 cm.). Joseph Blackburn painted this likeness in 1760, thirty years after Wentworth's death; the earlier life portrait from which it was probably copied is now lost. Merchant and sea captain as well as lieutenant governor, Wentworth was a member of a distinguished New England family: both his son Benning and his grandson John were governors of New Hampshire after its separation from Massachusetts. Wealth and position are indicated by the richness of Wentworth's dress and the formality of his pose.*
Courtesy of the New Hampshire Historical Society, gift of Anne Wentworth Morss, Margaret Wentworth Whiting, and Constance Wentworth Dodge

The new standards of taste and design that evolved in the William and Mary period are handsomely demonstrated in the chamber (upstairs room) from the John Wentworth house, built in Portsmouth, New Hampshire (Figs. 20 and 22). Its woodwork dates from about 1700, and most of its furnishings are from the years just before and after that date.

The main staircase of this house, also in the collection, is a rare and exceptionally handsome survival (Figs. 25 and 26). Earlier, the upper floor of a house had been gained either by means of a ladder or, more commonly, by stairs immediately within the front entrance, set against the bricks of the central chimney and enclosed by a wall of unmolded vertical boards, or sheathing. Here that area has been opened up. The chimney is covered by attractive paneling that is also used for the soffit (the underside of the staircase) and for the walls of the entry. Bold moldings enframe the individual panels. The most distinctive feature of this steeply rising staircase with high treads is the ranks of unusual spiral-turned balusters that support the heavy molded handrails. It is perhaps the most impressive example of its kind to have survived from the William and Mary period. It is also an early harbinger of the development of the small entry into a central hallway with a large and prominent staircase—a feature that became a focal element of the house.

The Wentworth chamber has a higher ceiling and a good deal more space than the Hart Room, and its architectural features are more formally and deliberately treated. Structural elements—all of white pine—still intrude into the room, but two of the corner posts are neatly boxed in, the girts are

20

Fig. 20. Wentworth Room, *Portsmouth, New Hampshire, 1695–1700. The newest fashions in American paneling and furnishing appear in this second-floor chamber from John Wentworth's house. With higher ceilings and fewer exposed posts and beams, this room brings us closer to the elegancies of eighteenth-century interiors. The variety of new forms signals the arrival of a new era too, for each specialized form makes the specific occupation for which it was designed a little easier. The dressing table, for example, has three handy drawers and an uncluttered surface on which to arrange powder, hairpins, and other necessities of the toilet. The couch, or daybed, serves as a sitting place by day and an extra bed by night. Using the same green fabric for the couch and other seating furniture as well as for the curtains was a practice that added a note of formality and a feeling of unity to the room. Although there are no surviving pictures to show us how rooms were arranged in America during the late seventeenth and early eighteenth centuries, European prints and paintings of that period depict interiors with all furniture not in use arranged around the walls. Since the colonists followed European furnishing conventions, we know that such room arrangements were customary in America too.*

Sage Fund, 1926 (26.290)

Fig. 21. Lantern clock, *England, about 1700; brass, height 14½ inches (36.8 cm.). Advertisements in the earliest colonial newspapers stating that old clocks could be "turn'd into Pendelums" indicate that a revolution had occurred in clock-making: the addition of a pendulum, invented in 1657, made timepieces much more accurate. Even so, the single hand on this example indicates that seventeenth-century Americans didn't feel the need to be punctual to the minute. The high arching top and boldly scrolled fret of the clock case echo other arches and scrolls throughout the room. A triangular projection on either side of the face allows the pendulum to swing freely back and forth. Only wealthy colonists could own imported accessories like this.* Gift of Mrs. J. Insley Blair, 1942 (42.197.11)

Fig. 22. Wentworth Room, *Portsmouth, New Hampshire, 1695–1700. Raised, or fielded, panels surrounded by bolection moldings achieve a splendid boldness on the fireplace wall. Among the new forms that appeared during the William and Mary period are the six-legged high chest, the gateleg table, and the easy chair, and all imply a heightened concern with personal comfort and convenience. This was the best chamber, or bedroom—equal to the parlor in elegance and formality—and it would also have contained a richly hung bed. Since the collection does not contain an appropriate bed, the room is furnished to give a feeling for the variety of high-style forms and accessories available to prosperous colonists in about 1700. Among the signs of affluence are*

21

22

the imported clock, blue and white ceramics, and Turkey carpet—the latter placed proudly on and not under the table. It was many years before such valuable weavings covered the floor.
Sage Fund, 1926 (26.290)

23

24

Fig. 23. Iron back, probably New England, about 1703; cast iron, 27¼ by 29 inches (69.2 by 73.7 cm.). A fort bristling with business-like cannons is depicted here. The determined figure atop the central bastion is possibly Joseph Dudley, governor of Massachusetts from 1702 to 1715. Above him flies the British flag. Iron backs served both to protect the brickwork of the fireplace and to reflect heat from the fire into the room. The high arching curve of the top of this example is the same as that found on the crest rails, stretchers, and arched skirts of furniture in the Wentworth Room.
Gift of Mrs. J. Insley Blair, 1947 (47.103.15)

deeply and decoratively chamfered, and the ceiling joists are concealed by plaster. The gunstock shape of the two remaining corner posts provides a substantial bearing for the crosswise girts.

The fireplace wall (Fig. 22), like the walls of the stairway, is composed of wide panels with heavy moldings. The fireplace opening is itself framed by a robust bolection (projecting) molding and is capped by a boldly fashioned mantel. Within the fireplace old bricks are laid in a herringbone pattern copied from a surviving example of the period—another instance of the deliberate attention to decorative detail that increasingly characterized American architecture of the early eighteenth century (see also Figs. 25–36).

Double-hung sash windows with molded muntins (narrow wooden strips that divide panes) were introduced into America very late in the seventeenth century and have remained a standard treatment. Here the windows are still relatively small and have no side hangings, but they have been fitted with draw curtains that follow a fashionable design of the period. When they are raised the curtains admit a maximum amount of daylight. Contemporary brass door hardware—box locks fitted with their original knobs and keys—replace the shapely wrought-iron fixtures seen in the Hart Room.

The new fashions of the William and Mary period are appropriately featured in the Wentworth Room. Oak furniture all but disappears and is replaced by lighter forms of walnut, maple, and similar hardwoods. A six-legged maple-veneered highboy is paired with a lowboy, or dressing table, a custom that became more or less conventional at this time and persisted for years. A group of

tall-backed William and Mary chairs with cushions of matching fabric and trimming further embody the sense of order and formality that was becoming a ruling principle in domestic arrangements. When they were not needed in other places, chairs were arranged against the wall, a practice that was customary until the nineteenth century.

Throughout the early years of the eighteenth century, Turkey "carpitts" were used as table rather than floor coverings by those who could afford such imported luxuries. The carpet was often laid over a gateleg table, a space-saving form that came into fashion during the William and Mary period. Its two large drop leaves, when raised, are supported by movable legs hinged to swing out from the fixed central frame. Tin-glazed pottery from Holland and England (broadly referred to as delftware) and such other imported items as looking glasses and small brass wall clocks became increasingly common accessories in well-to-do households (Figs. 20 and 21). Chinese porcelains that found their way to the wealthier American homes and silver plate fashioned both at home and abroad also testify to the colonies' growing affluence.

Fig. 24. Jug, German, 1680–1700; stoneware, 2¹⁵⁄₁₆ by 2⁹⁄₁₆ inches (7.5 by 6.5 cm.). Large numbers of gray salt-glazed stoneware pots, mugs, and jugs were exported from Germany to England and then to America during the seventeenth and eighteenth centuries. This jug, with its elaborate molded rosette pattern and blue background, is from the Westerwald region of Germany, where potters specialized in such decoration. The durable yet decorative Westerwald wares were widely used in colonial homes and taverns and are the ancestors of our own American blue-decorated gray stonewares of the nineteenth century.
Sansbury-Mills Fund, 1980 (1980.151)

Figs. 25–36. *This group of vigorous turnings, moldings, and carvings shows that the same characteristic shapes appear in both the architecture and the decorative arts of the William and Mary period. Stretchers, crest rails, banisters, legs, and feet repeat and reinforce the robust profiles of wall and fireplace moldings. Juxtaposed highlights and shadows, swells and tapers, curves and straight lines, and solids and voids relate these diverse elements even though the formula is different in each case.*
Figs. 25, 26: Rogers Fund, 1926 (26.290); *Figs. 27, 28:* Gift of Mrs. Screven Lorillard, 1952 (52.195.8); *Figs. 29, 30:* Gift of Mrs. Russell Sage, 1909 (10.125.678); *Figs. 31, 32:* Sage Fund, 1926 (26.290); *Figs. 33, 34:* Gift of Mrs. Russell Sage, 1909 (10.125.133); *Figs. 35, 36:* Gift of Mrs. Russell Sage, 1909 (10.125.704)

25

Fig. 25. Wentworth Stair, *Portsmouth, New Hampshire, 1695–1700. Twist balusters and boldly molded paneled walls enrich this small hallway. Before the advent of the center hall, stair entries like this were squeezed between the massive center chimney and the front door. These are the earliest twist-turned balusters known in New England.*
Rogers Fund, 1926 (26.290)

26

27

28

29

30

31

32

33

34

35

36

Hewlett Room

As the seventeenth century waned, more and more new elements were introduced into architecture. Renaissance influence found its earliest significant expression in America in the better houses then being built. Although most of them have disappeared or been altered beyond recognition, it was these houses, with their emphasis on symmetry and formal order, their uses of classical and baroque motifs, and their interior arrangements, that introduced the elements of style and comfort that prevailed throughout the remainder of the colonial period.

A tentative approach to such refinements is apparent in the Wentworth Room. Interiors from the mid-eighteenth century illustrate how the new modes were interpreted in different areas of the New England and New York countryside. More sophisticated developments are displayed in the late-colonial period rooms.

In the interior from the Metcalf Bowler house, built near Newport, Rhode Island, about 1763, we meet for the first time in the Wing features that recall, modestly but pleasantly, the formal practices of the Georgian architecture of England. These had been introduced into the colonies by English building and architectural manuals—manuals that were adapted from Renaissance publications that were in turn interpretations of classical designs of antiquity. Throughout most of the eighteenth century this classical spirit thrice removed was a persistent influence on American architecture, both exterior and interior, and this is evident in all the rest of the colonial rooms in the Wing.

For example, the woodwork of a room salvaged from the John Hewlett house, built at Woodbury, Long Island,

about 1740–60 (Fig. 38), reflects the influence of English manuals. Fluted pilasters carried up into projections of the cornice represent in provincial fashion a classical entablature although, to be sure, it is not clearly understood (Fig. 37). In the Hart Room the structural needs of the house, frankly stated, made the "style." In this case the applied designs largely obscure the underlying framework of the house. The abbreviated pilasters over the fireplace, for example, rest on nothing and do not even suggest structural supports.

Dutch tiles painted under the glaze with scriptural subjects surround the fireplace opening (Fig. 44). Such decorative borders were advertised for sale in colonial newspapers from the early days of the eighteenth century. The fireplace is flanked by a shell-carved "beaufett," or cupboard, for the display of pottery, glassware, and other useful and decorative accessories. The room is painted a bright blue that painstaking analysis indicates was its original color. In 1748 the visiting Swedish naturalist Peter Kalm noted that blue was a usual interior-wall color in New York. Blue and white resist-dyed fabric was apparently widely used in and about New York for bed and window hangings and upholstery (Fig. 42).

A painted cupboard, or *kas*, from the New York area is a delightful reminder of the huge Dutch prototypes whose expensive woods and ornate carvings are here simulated by grisaille decoration painted on the pine carcass (Figs. 43 and 45). Such representations of fruit and vegetable forms could be considered the earliest American still-life painting.

A chair also characteristic of the New York area from Long Island to Albany

37

38

Figs. 39–41. Chairs from, left to right, *Pennsylvania or New Jersey, New York, and New England, 1730–80; maple, painted, height 48¾ inches (123.8 cm.); maple, painted, height 40¾ inches (103.5 cm.); and maple, ash, height 41½ inches (105.4 cm.).* Everywhere in the colonies seats that could be made quickly and bought cheaply were in demand, and chairmakers responded with different versions that have become characteristic of their regions. The Delaware River valley turned out a slat-back chair whose most characteristic features are graceful slats that curve upward at both top and bottom, rear stiles that taper slightly from foot to finial, prominent turned front stretchers, and onion-like turned finials and front feet. Hudson River valley makers produced a broad-splatted, chubby-legged chair with pad feet that rest on disks; this type was also popular in New Jersey, on Long Island, and in Connecticut, where it was referred to as a "York" chair because people associated it with New York. New Englanders, like New Yorkers, combined William and Mary and Queen Anne features in their inexpensive chairs. This example differs from its York cousin in having a serpentine curved back, a narrower splat, and block-and-vase turned front legs.

Purchase, Virginia Groomes Gift, in memory of Mary W. Groomes, 1975 (1975.310); Rogers Fund, 1933 (33.121.1); Gift of Mrs. Russell Sage, 1909 (10.125.263)

42

39

40

41

49

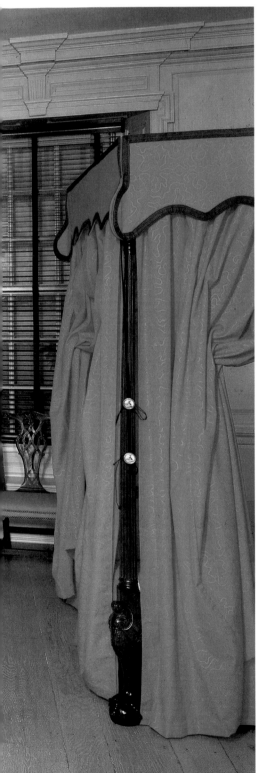

Ｎew England furniture was often shipped to the southern colonies, and examples of such northern exports have been installed in a room taken from a brick house known as Almodington in Somerset County, Maryland (Fig. 48). The walls of this interior, divided horizontally by a heavy chair rail, are paneled from floor to ceiling in a manner that was gradually going out of fashion by the middle of the eighteenth century. The present mantelpiece replaced an earlier one about 1814. The shell-top cupboards on either side of the fireplace might have contained Delft from Holland, salt-glazed wares from England, and possibly China Trade porcelains, all of which added decorative emphasis to many rooms of the time and, to be sure, also saw active use at dining and tea tables (Fig. 49). A painting on the wall, attributed to Copley, could be his original oil sketch for *Brook Watson and the Shark* (Fig. 52). This is the canvas that, when shown at the Royal Academy in London shortly after Copley had taken up his permanent residence abroad, was hailed as among the "first performances" of that prestigious exhibition.

The room is furnished as a gentleman's bedroom. The most conspicuous piece of furniture in it is a Boston-made four-posted bedstead with cabriole legs on the footposts that have detachable carved kneecaps and that terminate in boldly shaped claw-and-ball feet (Fig. 51). The bed hangings and the upholstery on an attendant easy chair and a suite of side chairs—also made in Boston—are all cut from the same stout cloth, a raspberry red wool moreen embossed in a vermicelli pattern (so named because it resembles a formal arrangement of strands of thin spaghetti). Both

50

Fig. 50. Candlestand, inscribed by Benjamin Gerrish (about 1686–1750), Boston, about 1735; iron and brass, height 49¼ inches (125.7 cm.). *Delicate wrought-iron standing candle holders are rare, and signed examples are even rarer. This and one other stand, dated 1736, are signed by Benjamin Gerrish, gunsmith and brazier of Cambridge and Boston. The two candles held by this stand produced lavish illumination by eighteenth-century standards, when many households depended on the flickering flames of the fire to light the room,*
Rogers Fund, 1920 (20.110)

Fig. 51. Bedstead, *detail, Massachusetts, 1760–90; mahogany, height 89 inches (226.1 cm.). One of the surest signs of wealth in the eighteenth century was an impressive bed. The fluted footposts and carved legs and feet of this example are admirable, and the richly carved detachable kneecaps, added to conceal the bolts that join the side and foot rails, are particularly rare. The bedstead is one of a very small group of Massachusetts examples with such kneecaps. Their elegance is indisputable, but their precise origin is as yet unknown. However, the sharply raked side talons of the claw that grasps the ball foot is a feature that is associated with the finest furniture produced in eastern Massachusetts.*
Gift of Mrs. Russell Sage, 1909 (10.125.336)

Fig. 52. Brook Watson and the Shark, *by John Singleton Copley (1738–1815), 1782; oil on canvas, 24⅞ by 30⅛ inches (63.2 by 76.5 cm.). Most eighteenth-century American paintings are portraits, not historical scenes like this. The subject, Brook Watson being attacked by a shark in Havana harbor, was based on an actual occurrence. Watson lost part of one leg to the shark, and is shown being rescued just in time to prevent loss of the other leg. The painting is undeniably dramatic, but is unusual for its time in depicting a scene that, though vivid, has no marked historical importance.*
Gift of Mrs. Gordon Dexter, 1942 (42.71.1)

the pattern and the color are exact reproductions of eighteenth-century samples. Contemporary references to "the red room" or "the green room" indicate that as often as not a single fabric, or hue at least, served throughout a room, as it does here. Appropriately, a dressing table and a dressing glass stand between the windows (Fig. 53). A highboy or a chest-on-chest like the one against the wall opposite these windows served for the storage of wearing apparel, linens, and so forth in a day when closets were not yet common conveniences.

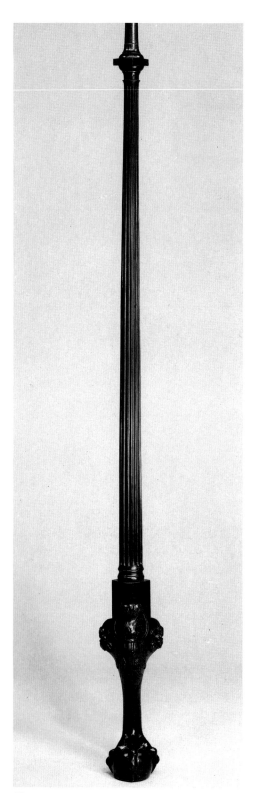

51

52

Fig. 53. Dressing glass with drawers, *Boston, 1760–90; mahogany, white pine, height 32½ inches (82.6 cm.). In an era before "the modern bureau with its expansive glass, capable of reflecting everything in the room except the hang of one's nether garments" had come into prominence, this sort of small standing mirror, with or without drawers, provided a convenient glass to use while making up. Meant to sit atop a dressing table as it does here, this glass incorporates a feature characteristic of a small group of the very highest-style Boston pieces—the bombé base. For reasons that are still unknown, the bombé, or kettle-shaped, form caught on in Boston and its immediate environment and provided a surprisingly baroque note in an otherwise staid group of case pieces. Its use in a dressing box is very rare.*
Bequest of Cecile L. Mayer, 1962 (62.171.14)

53

Powel Room

A parlor from a house built in Philadelphia about 1765 and owned by Samuel Powel, the last colonial mayor of that city, incorporates a rich display of scrupulously executed ornament drawn from contemporary English pattern books (Fig. 54). These highly decorative designs represent a culmination of the advanced stylistic trends of the late colonial period. Powel had traveled widely and was abreast of the latest fashions from abroad. He had made the grand tour of Europe, during the course of which he was presented to George III and to the king of Sardinia. In Rome he had numerous conversations with the duke of York and on his journey back from Italy he paid a visit to Voltaire.

Powel was also wealthy enough to command the finest craftsmanship in

Fig. 54. Powel Room, Philadelphia; built 1765–66, remodeled 1769–71. The original use of the Museum's room—one of the two finest in the Powel house—is not known. It is seen here furnished as a parlor, with the numerous chairs and tables indicated as parlor furniture by eighteenth-century wills and inventories. The room contains some of the finest surviving carved woodwork of the late colonial period but, not content with the beautiful chimney breast and cornice, the curators who installed this room in the 1920s copied the elaborate ceiling design of the ballroom, the room originally next to this one on the second floor of the Powel house. To add further richness, they hung the walls with sumptuous hand-painted Chinese wallpaper, which is of the period but was not originally on these walls. Perhaps, knowing of the brilliant social events that took place in the Powel rooms, the curators were striving to create surroundings worthy of such luminaries as George Washington, who was a frequent visitor. Their additions have been retained by the current staff as a tribute to the taste and vision of collectors and scholars of the twenties, for they have had an enduring effect on later generations' views of the American past.
Rogers Fund, 1918 (18.87.1–4)

54

55

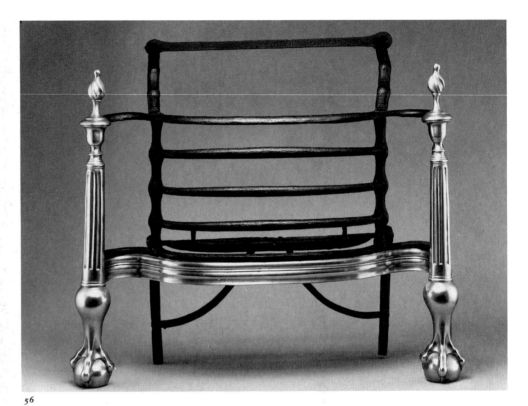

56

furbishing his elegant town house. The carved and molded decoration of the wood- and plasterwork are masterly interpretations of the style associated with Chippendale's adaptations of French rococo designs. The plaster relief of the ceiling, in a pattern of swags, flowers, musical trophies, and pendent masks in the French manner, is a cast taken from the ceiling of an adjoining room in the same house.

By now the fireplace, which in the earliest days of colonization had been in effect a hole cut in the fabric of the house for utility's sake, had become the most formally featured element of interior architecture. It was indeed the focus of a principal room, and in this age of highly stylized design it and what is termed chimney furniture were treated with full regard for their decorative quality and interest. The carving on the

overmantel resembles that which distinguishes fine Philadelphia furniture of the period. English statuettes on the mantelpiece include a fine one of John Wilkes, whose outspoken sympathy in the British Parliament for the American cause won him the gratitude of colonial patriots (Fig. 59).

Wilkes was far from being the only Englishman who supported the colonists in their grievances during the years immediately preceding the Revolution—and during the war itself. The people of the mother country were worried enough about their own liberties at that time (see Fig. 420). When Parliament was obliged to repeal the odious Stamp Act in 1766, one London artist made a small fortune satirizing the defeat of Parliament in a cartoon that was sold for sixpence and that was pirated in at least a half-dozen versions by rival

printsellers. (The original artist was Benjamin Wilson, whose portrait of Franklin was taken from his home as booty by Major André when the British evacuated Philadelphia, carried back to England, and finally returned—to the White House—in 1906.)

Within the overmantel hangs Charles Willson Peale's portrait of Mrs. Thomas Harwood of Maryland, probably completed about 1771. One authority has written that this painting is "the most vivid and charming of Peale's portraits of women, a personification of feminine grace and dignity." (For the fascinating story of Peale's many-sided career, see p. 295.)

Three walls of the room are covered with Chinese wallpaper that originally hung in another house of the same period. Such exotic wall coverings enjoyed a vogue among the fashionable gentry of the time. Robert Morris, Powel's cousin and the chief financier of the Revolution, ordered a set for his own sumptuous home, but for some reason never got around to hanging it. Copies and approximations of Chinese papers were made in England and these also found their way to America. Thomas Hancock ordered a set from London for a room in his very elegant Beacon Hill house, sending as a pattern a sample of a wallpaper that had recently been installed in the house of one of his wealthy friends and that, he wrote, "takes much in ye Town. . . . Get mine well Done & as Cheap as Possible, & if they can make it more Beautifull by adding more Birds flying here & there, with Some Landskip at the Bottom, should Like it well. . . ." By way of further advice to his agent Hancock continued, "In other of these hangings are great variety of different Sorts of Birds, Peacocks, Macoys, Squirril, Monkys, Fruit and Flowers, etc.," and he said he hoped his order might be executed by the same hand that had created his friend's model of fashion.

Here, as in so many other contemporary examples, the eclectic character of eighteenth-century design and decoration reveal the widening horizons of colonial culture. Within a house of typical Georgian style, its exterior arrangement reflecting Renaissance precedents drawn from classical sources (Fig. 55), individual rooms might display baroque broken pediments, decorative oriental features, and rococo embellishments derived from French sources, all agreeably and sensitively combined.

A unique series of paintings in the Chinese manner with scenes of the Buddhist hell, Chinese courts of punishment, and some more ordinary oriental birds and flowers was applied directly on the plaster walls of the parlor in a Newport house that Metcalf Bowler acquired as his city residence in 1759. The ingenious artist who created these fanciful chinoiseries has never been identified. For some reason of fashion they were at one point covered by wooden paneling, and were not rediscovered until 1937.

The brass-and-iron coal-burning fire grate was probably made in the colonies (Fig. 56). As early as 1667 the records of one New England community complained "that great waste is made in the

Fig. 57. Side chair, Philadelphia, 1760–90; mahogany, height 46½ inches (118.1 cm.). The modern name "strap splat" is sometimes applied to this type of chair back because the solid Queen Anne splat of the previous period has been carved into interlaced curved "straps" to make a graceful design. Here the straps are enriched by leaf carving, a decorative tassel provides a focal point for the central void, and flowing leafage and a sculptural shell enrich the boldly scrolled crest rail. Shells and leaves ornament the front seat-rail and legs, and stop fluting emphasizes the verticality of the rear stiles. This was one of the most popular Philadelphia chair-back patterns, though this example is especially richly ornamented. Tassel-back chairs were also produced in

New York, Massachusetts, and Charleston. The Sylmaris Collection, Gift of George Coe Graves, 1932 (32.57.2)

57

Fig. 58. Stand table, Philadelphia, 1760–90; *mahogany, height 28¼ inches (71.8 cm.). This lovely little table is both unusual, in being smaller than most others of its type, and typical, in having a round top supported by a turned column on a tripod base. During the late colonial period this was the preferred form for fashionable Philadelphia tea tables, and they bore as much or as little carved ornament as suited the customer's taste and pocketbook. The carving here is plentiful and particularly fine, enriching the eight-lobed "piecrust" top, the turned column, and the sinuous cabriole legs.*
John Stewart Kennedy Fund, 1918 (18.110.44)

58

wood and timber in the Common Lands of the Throne," which was judged "very prejudiciall at present but especially for the succeeding generations which it concerne us to consider." There was then, of course, no visible end to the supply of firewood in the colonies. But as the forest receded from growing communities, wood gatherers had to go increasing distances for their harvests, and the cost of haulage mounted accordingly. In 1737 growing alarm over the continued recession of the forests led to the first proposal for conservation in this country, an alarm that has a typical ring in our own day. By the middle of the eighteenth century one contemporary reported that coal was now being increasingly used "both for kitchen fires and in other rooms."

All the furniture in the Powel Room is fashioned in the sophisticated version of the Chippendale style that was popular among the affluent gentry of Philadelphia and its environs. Between the two windows a tall, elaborately framed pier glass with gilded carving is hung above a slab table. A number of side and armchairs with carved splats of varying popular patterns (Fig. 57) complement a tilt-top table and a tripod stand, both supported by carved cabriole legs (Figs. 54 and 58). Such graceful forms were generally used for serving tea, which had by now become a formal social ritual that called for this and other special equipment. A handsome mahogany desk further contributes to the elegance that so deeply impressed John Adams when he first visited the homes of Philadelphians on the eve of the Revolution. To the staid New Englander Powel's "splendid seat," and his hosting a "most sinfull Feast" with an abundance of delicacies of all sorts, smacked of

Fig. 59. Figure of John Wilkes, Derby, England, 1770–75; soft-paste porcelain, height 12¾ inches (32.4 cm). Although "burnt images and figures for mantelpieces" were a rarity even in wealthy pre-Revolutionary homes, the Powels' house, with its elegant parties and illustrious company, was as likely a place for these charming luxuries as any in the colonies. The figure shown here is of John Wilkes, a staunch defender of liberty for all Englishmen, including colonists, and he became something of a hero during the American Revolution. George III was so outraged by Wilkes's published criticism of the crown's policies that he had the author thrown into jail more than once.
Fletcher Fund, 1944 (44.89.2)

Fig. 60. Desk and bookcase, detail, Philadelphia, 1765–90; mahogany. One of the chief glories of the Chippendale period in America was high-style Philadelphia furniture. The combination of richly grained mahogany masses and free-flowing rococo carving worked particularly well on large pieces such as high chests and desks and bookcases. An impressive group within this category is ornamented with three-dimensional portrait busts (see desk and bookcase, left, Fig. 54), of which this female figure is an example. She appears to have been taken from a plate in Thomas Chippendale's famous design book, The Gentleman and Cabinet-Maker's Director, first published in London in 1754. The modeling of this bust is considerably more deep and detailed

than that of another such bust in the collection—the one nicknamed "Madame Pompadour" that graces the extraordinary high chest shown in Fig. 187.
Rogers Fund, 1918 (18.110.1)

59

60

prodigality. Washington, another of Powel's many distinguished guests, was less awed by these surroundings and the ample hospitality they offered. At the Powels' on one occasion at least, he romped through a succession of dances with a number of younger ladies as his wife, Martha, who no longer danced, looked on—benignly, we can only hope. Nevertheless, it was reported that the "luxury and profusion" with which he was there surrounded gave the general "infinitely more pain than pleasure."

The elegance of this and other rooms could hardly be imagined from the outside of the house. As the population of colonial urban centers increased rapidly, building space became restricted, and in the central sections of the larger cities houses were built in rows of adjoining or closely spaced structures. The Powel house, built in 1765–66 by Charles Stedman and sold to Powel in 1769, is an example of such a house. It still stands at 244 South Third Street, restored by the Philadelphia Society for the Preservation of Landmarks.

Van Rensselaer Hall

Interiors from other geographical areas provide the opportunity to compare and contrast regional characteristics. A large and magnificent entry hall comes from the Van Rensselaer manor house, built at Albany, New York, between 1765 and 1769 by Stephen Van Rensselaer II (Fig. 61). The house was one of the most important examples of Georgian architecture in the middle Atlantic colonies.

The patroonship of Rensselaerwyck, which in 1637 had been granted by the Dutch administration to Kiliaen Van Rensselaer, a pearl merchant from Amsterdam, stretched for twenty-four miles on either side of the Hudson River in the vicinity of Fort Orange (Albany). In 1685, twenty-one years after the British take-over of New Amsterdam, this vast area became the manor of Rensselaerwyck. As a footnote to history, Stephen's son and namesake was to be "the last of the patroons." When he died in 1839, in the aftermath of Andrew Jackson's turbulent democratic upheaval, the spectacle of a landed gentleman living in semifeudal splendor among the 3,000 tenants who worked his 700,000 acres had become an insupportable anachronism. The estate was broken up and in time the great house was dismantled. Elements of its central hall came to the Museum from descendants of the patroons.

More than forty-six feet long and twenty-three feet wide, this extravagantly embellished and monumental high-ceilinged room offers a spectacular contrast to the tiny entrance halls of earlier colonial dwellings. Originally this hall ran from the front to the rear entrance, with a stairway to the upper story through an arch at one side. The intricate rococo carving in the spandrels

61

72

Fig. 73. Detail of Marmion wall painting,
1770–80. This charming cornucopia is one of the rococo motifs that blend with neoclassical ones to ornament the walls of the Marmion Room. Since it shows considerable joie de vivre, but somewhat less skill in execution than the imaginary scene over the fireplace, it may be the work of a different hand.
Rogers Fund, 1916 (16.112)

O ne of the most interesting of all surviving early American domestic interiors is that from Marmion, the Virginia plantation home of the Fitzhugh family (Figs. 72 and 74). Here the architectural treatment of Ionic pilasters and entablature conforms with unusual fidelity to the Renaissance conception of the classical order (Fig. 71). Part of the woodwork is painted to simulate marble; the larger wall panels show landscapes suggestive of Dutch painting, representations of urns with flowers (Fig. 71), festoons of leaves, and asymmetrical scrolls. These may be the work of one of the itinerant artists who advertised in newspapers that they could do all sorts of paintings, including landscapes "in the neatest Manner." The Siena-marble-lined corner fireplace is thus placed to enable the end chimney to serve two fireplaces on each floor of the house.

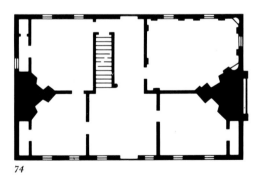
74

Fig. 74. Plan of Marmion, *showing the central hall with two rooms opening off either side. This became the standard arrangement for Virginia houses, first for the large ones and then for the smaller ones as well. The Museum's room is paneled with woodwork from the large back parlor on the right in this plan.*

The Federal Period, 1790–1820

75

***Fig. 75.* The Prodigal Son Revelling with Harlots,** *by Amos Doolittle (1754–1832), 1814; engraving, 14 by 10⅜ inches (35.6 by 26.4 cm.). Although Doolittle may have been inspired by contemporary English engravings of a similar subject, he set the scene in his own New England, providing us with fascinating details of dress and interior decoration during the Federal period.* Gift of Mrs. J. Insley Blair, 1948 (48.95.2)

I n the several decades following the Revolutionary War, years that are broadly referred to as the Federal period, fresh currents of taste and design flowed into the new republic from European countries, notably England and France. The convulsions of the war had delayed the appearance of these new trends in America, and by the time they appeared here they had become firmly rooted abroad. A second classical revival was taking place—this time based not on Renaissance concepts, as in the earlier Georgian period, but on a more direct and accurate knowledge of ancient art and architecture. Among other remains scattered throughout the Mediterranean world and accessible for study by archeologically minded adventurers were the recently excavated ruins of Pompeii and Herculaneum. Suddenly buried (and preserved) under ash from the volcanic eruption of Mount Vesuvius in the first century A.D., these cities provided a new vocabulary of ornament and decoration that was translated into the delicate neoclassical styles of France and England.

The architect-designers Robert Adam and his brother James were the foremost English exponents of this fashion. Their *Works in Architecture,* published at London in 1773–79, had an electric effect on the development of both architecture and the decorative arts. Robert Adam had toured Italy and Dalmatia, carefully studying classical remains at first hand. With the designs he created after his return to England, his professed aim was "to transfuse the beautiful spirit of antiquity with novelty and variety." This he did in highly personal fashion, including in his proposals every kind of household equipment from inkstands and fire grates to sideboards and bookcases, as well as architecture. These light and graceful adaptations of ancient Roman ornament quickly won him the patronage of wealthy and aristocratic clients throughout the British Isles.

In fashionable American houses of the Federal period, rooms tended to be more spacious than ever before and to have higher ceilings and larger windows (which sometimes extended, French style, to the floor). In 1790, when Abigail Adams was living in New York while that city was the new nation's temporary capital, she wrote her sister that all the rooms of her present residence were eleven feet high, which caused her some inconvenience in furnishing it adequately. Oval, round, and octagonal rooms added variety to floor plans. (The oval room of the White House is a historic example.) By the end of the eighteenth century the up-to-date American home might have had numerous rooms for special purposes—a dining room, a parlor, a library, a ballroom, as well as kitchen and bedrooms (but rarely a bathroom)—creating a domestic environment far removed from the all-purpose seventeenth-century hall, and calling for furnishings of a different order from those of the colonial period.

Haverhill Room

Fig. 76. Bedstead, *Boston, 1808–12; mahogany with painted and gilded cornice, height 106¾ inches (271.1 cm.). Bedstead attributed to workshop of Thomas Seymour (active 1794–1843); carving attributed to Thomas Whitman (active 1809); cornice attributed to John Doggett (1780–1857); painted decoration attributed to John Penniman (active 1806–28). This bedstead is said to have been made for Elizabeth, daughter of Elias Hasket Derby, one of the grandest and wealthiest of New England's merchant princes, and if its richness and excellent workmanship are any indication, it was. It is the finest of a very select group of carved, painted, and gilded bedsteads made in Salem and Boston whose inspiration seems to have been Thomas Sheraton's design* for a similar bed in the Appendix *to his* Drawing Book *(Pl. 9, London, 1802). The group of artisans who cooperated to produce this bedstead includes some of the most talented craftsmen of the period, and this is a most interesting instance of such cooperation among specialists to produce a masterpiece.*

John Stewart Kennedy Fund, 1918 (18.110.64)

oston's North Shore was an area where superb craftsmen found ample and discriminating patronage during the Federal period. For more than a generation after the Revolution Salem was one of the celebrated ports of the world. Its seamen, wrote one historian, "were despatched to every part of the world, and to every nook of barbarism which had a market and a shore." In some remote areas where its ships seemed everywhere to be seen it was believed that the small town *was* the United States—an immensely rich and important country. As another historian has written, the list of exotic freight brought home to Salem conjures up an oriental bazaar—ivory and gold dust from Guinea, gum copal from Zanzibar, iron from Gothenburg and St. Petersburg, coffee and palm oil from Arabia, whale oil from the Antarctic, silks and pepper from the Far East, hemp from Luzon, hides from the Rio de la Plata, silk slippers from somewhere east of Good Hope, and among the interminable variety of other things, one elephant in good condition, the first to be seen in America.

Merchants in Salem and neighboring towns grew wealthy from their foreign ventures, and their demands for the best in houses and furnishings were ably met by the consummate craftsmen of the area. Visible evidence of their good fortune endures in their dwellings and in the furniture that was made for them. An interior with woodwork from the Duncan house, built twenty miles from Salem in Haverhill, Massachusetts, about 1805, is furnished as the bed-sitting room of a New England merchant prince (Fig. 77). Details such as thin, reeded columns with brass bases and capitals on the mantel, plaster or-

76

Fig. 77. Haverhill Room, *Haverhill, Massachusetts, about 1805. After the Revolutionary War, New Englanders sailed off to the four corners of the globe, trading as they went. Many made large fortunes, and it was not unusual for a man of thirty to retire from the sea, leaving the sailing and trading to his employees. The wealthy young man was then free to build himself a fine house and fill it with the best of everything. The Haverhill Room is arranged to show what luxurious and elegant objects were available to furnish the bed-sitting room of a New England merchant prince. Furniture echoes the symmetry and delicacy, straight lines and geometrical shapes of the newly fashionable Federal architecture, and among the new forms that appeared* were those represented by the sewing or worktable at the end of the bed, the washstand in the corner, and the girandole mirror over the mantel. Beside the fireplace is an easy chair whose symmetrical serpentine curves and straight tapered legs are typical of this form in the early neoclassical period. While it contrasts markedly with the delicacy of everything else in the room, the wall-to-wall ingrain carpet with its bold geometrical pattern of squares and crosses is of a type that was popular throughout most of the nineteenth century.
Rogers Fund, 1912 (12.121)

Fig. 78. Side chair, detail, Boston, 1795–1810; bird's-eye and striped maple. Part of a set of fourteen that descended in John Hancock's family, these unusual square-backed chairs express the spirit of neoclassicism in general and of New England neoclassicism in particular. The design of ovals within a square is in the early Federal tradition of strict symmetry. The shape of the square back is emphasized at each corner by a smaller square enclosing a carved rosette on a punchwork ground. The use of light woods with a rich grain is characteristic of northern New England.
Lent by Kaufman Americana Foundation
(L.1979.26.1)

78

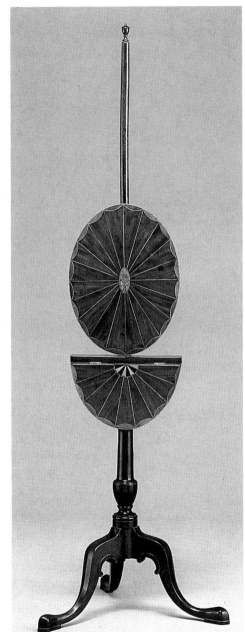

nament on the chair rail and chimney breast, and cornice with fret design copied from the 1792 edition of William Pain's *Builder's Companion* combine to produce a harmonious early nineteenth-century North Shore interior. The room is dominated by what is generally considered the finest surviving American bed from this period—a magnificent joint accomplishment of thoroughly proficient craftsmen that descended in the Derby family (Fig. 76). Its cornice, original in conception and decorated in colors and gold, was the combined achievement of John Doggett, a celebrated looking-glass-frame maker of Roxbury, Massachusetts, and John Ritto Penniman, an ornamental painter who, along with other gifted artisans, worked with Doggett on some of his many commissions. The bedstead itself was fashioned in the workshop of Thomas Seymour; the exquisitely carved details on the foot posts are attributed to Thomas Whitman.

Fig. 79. Pole screen with hinged shelf, Salem, 1785–95; mahogany, holly and ebony inlays, height 61½ inches (156.2 cm.). Elegant little forms like this indicate America's prosperity in the second half of the eighteenth century. Only a household that was completely fitted up with the necessities would contain such a luxury as a pole, or fire, screen—it was an extra, an expensive nicety that made life more comfortable. The purpose of such a screen was to shield the person next to it from the heat and glare of the fire. This example has, in addition, a folding shelf for a candle, a refinement found only on the finest examples. The style of this screen is transitional—it combines the snake feet of the Chippendale period with the oval screen and inlay of the Federal era.
Gift of Mrs. A. Goodwin Cooke, in memory of her mother, Mrs. Frederic C. Munroe, and Purchase, Anonymous Gift and Friends of the American Wing Fund, 1977 (1977.425)

79

Baltimore Room

80

Fig. 80. Urn, one of a pair, China, 1785–
1815; porcelain, height 16³/16 (41.5 cm.). The
symmetrical pistol-handled urn form and its
idealized landscape in an oval are characteristic
of neoclassical design. The antecedents of the
form are a late sixteenth-century Italian urn and,
more immediately, a late eighteenth-century version by the English potter Josiah Wedgwood. Such
oriental porcelains designed for the Western market were made in great numbers in the Federal
period when, for the first time, American ships began to make the long journey to Canton. Once
there, they traded goods that ranged from furs
and tobacco to ginseng for coveted Chinese tea,
silks, and ceramics.
Gift of Mrs. W. Murray Crane, 1954 (54.87.34)

By the beginning of the nineteenth
century the port of Baltimore,
commanding the shipping on Chesa-
peake Bay, had become a principal market town for most of the South and a
good portion of Pennsylvania. One European visitor commended the city's
"American frankness and French ease."
Its rocketing prosperity brought an in-
flux of skilled craftsmen, many from
Great Britain, and their work was more
English in character than that of any
other American city.

In the dining room removed from
a house built in Baltimore just before
the War of 1812 the architectural elements—pilasters, colonnettes, and cornice worked in solid pine—are all delicate in scale and refined in detail (Fig.
81). The relationships between the wall
openings—arched recesses flanking the
fireplace, windows, and doors—and the
wall surfaces, whose oval panels echo
those of the alcoves and the mantel, reveal a studied composition and a restrained elegance typical of the revived
classicism of the early republic.

In the center of the Baltimore Room
are a sectional dining table (Figs. 84 and
85) and a set of square-back Sheraton-
style chairs (Fig. 83) that exemplify the
regional characteristics of Baltimore
and of the mid-Atlantic or southern regions, respectively. On the card tables in
the arched recesses are a pair of beautifully colored and gilded urns (Fig. 80).
Above them a remarkably handsome
pair of carved and gilded Massachusetts
wall mirrors with *églomisé* inserts make it
evident that painted-glass decoration
was not exclusively a Baltimore device
(Fig. 82).

81

Fig. 81. Baltimore Room, *913 East Pratt Street, Baltimore, about 1810. "Some forty years ago," wrote the Russian diplomat Paul Svinin about 1812, Baltimore "consisted of several fishermen's huts. Now it is one of the fairest cities of North America, in point of wealth and trade occupying the first place after Philadelphia, New York, and Boston." The architecture and moldings of this Baltimore room are simple but elegant, emphasizing ovals and rectangles. The furniture is mainly from the Baltimore area, with imported accessories: the chandelier and candelabra are from England, the porcelain dinner service from France, and the pistol-handled urns were made in China for the Western market. The floor covering of such a room, however, might* either have been imported from England or made in America. This one is a reproduction floorcloth—a decorative but eminently practical alternative to a carpet or painted floor. Made of canvas or some other heavy cloth and covered with several layers of oil paint, floorcloths were remarkably durable. Charles Carroll of Annapolis certainly expected those he ordered from England in 1767 to stand up to hard wear, for he stipulated that they be able to "bear mopping over with a wet mop and Put up Dry and so as not to be Cracked or to have the Paint Rubbed of [f]."
Rogers Fund, 1918 (18.101.1–4)

83

Fig. 82. Looking glass, *one of a pair, Boston, 1795–1810; gilt gesso on pine and wire, églomisé tablet, height 50½ inches (128.3 cm.). Although églomisé decoration, or reverse painting on glass, is usually associated with Baltimore furniture, it was used by Boston and Salem craftsmen as well. Here it forms the central ornament of the upper mirror section of this extraordinarily decorative looking glass. Gilded vases of wheat sprays, pendent husks, and a splendid feathery eagle are executed with skill and combined to produce a supremely elegant object that, like the bedstead in the Haverhill Room, epitomizes the symmetry, delicacy, and refinement of the early Federal period.*
Sansbury-Mills Fund, 1956 (56.46.1)

Fig. 83. Square-back side chairs, *two of a set of ten, southern or mid-Atlantic states, 1795–1810; mahogany, heights 36¾ inches (93.4 cm.). Straight lines, square outlines, and chaste stylized ornament carved in low relief are features that place these seats in the early Federal period. The splat is composed of characteristic motifs—three feathers, drapery swags, and urn—used together here to create an unusual silhouette.*
Bequest of Flora E. Whiting, 1971 (1971.180.16–17)

Figs. 84 and 85. Dining table, *details, Baltimore, 1795–1810; mahogany, sycamore inlay. Between 1790 and 1810 Baltimore furniture was richly and distinctively ornamented. Inlay was particularly popular, and a light-wood "teardrop" used as a background for further inlay was a favorite device. The pendent husks, or bellflowers, that descend this teardrop are one of the best-known Baltimore motifs. Each petal is very clearly delineated, with the middle one unmistakably longer than the other two. The eagle in a patera, or oval inlay, is a simplified version of the bald eagle on the Great Seal of the newly formed United States of America.*
Rogers Fund, 1919 (19.13.1,2)

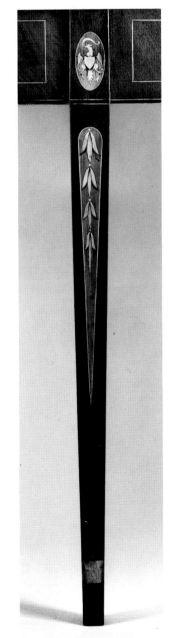

84

85

Richmond Room

Fig. 87. Richmond Room, *Richmond, Virginia, 1810. A new boldness has replaced the delicacy of proportion and restraint in scale and ornament that were principal characteristics of the Haverhill and Baltimore Rooms. Here both architecture and ornament have taken on a grand—even showy—aspect. Door and window openings are larger, made important by substantial friezes. The use of mahogany, an unusual but eminently suitable choice for an interior in this style, increases the impact of the woodwork; another unexpected choice is seen in the King of Prussia marble baseboards. Marble is used again for the mantel, whose caryatid supports and anthemion border are larger and more boldly sculptured than the linear Adamesque ornament of the earlier rooms. Furniture and accessories are suit-ably rich: mahogany, gilt bronze, and cut glass complement the woodwork and wallpaper. Since the French Empire style was a decided influence on its American counterpart, it is not surprising that the* bouillotte *lamp on the card table and the clock on the mantel are both French. Above the clock is a girandole mirror made in either England or America after a French design. The assertively figured Aubusson carpet carries out the theme of substantial classicism, but the wallpaper, a copy of a popular French pattern called "Monuments of Paris," supplies a lighter, more open feeling. The electric blue silk at the windows and on the sofa and chairs is a reproduction of the Chinese-export silk that originally covered these seats.*

Gift of Joe Kindig, Jr., 1968 (68.137)

86

Fig. 86. Clock, *works by Dubuc (active about 1780–1819), Paris, 1792–1819; bronze, gilded, height 19 inches (48.3 cm.). Like many other European artists and craftsmen, the firm of Dubuc produced goods especially for the American market, taking advantage of Americans' taste for objects whose ornament commemorated their new independence. This clock features George Washington in a pose borrowed from John Trumbull's painting* Washington Before the Battle of Trenton, *well known in Europe through engravings, and an American eagle perched on a globe. The frieze on the base shows Washington relinquishing his commission as commander in chief of the American army. The clock is inscribed "Dubuc/Rue Michel-le-Comte No. 33/A PARIS."*
Bequest of Jane E. Andrews, in memory of her husband, William Loring Andrews, 1930 (31.41.1)

 Examples of the work of leading New York cabinetmakers Phyfe and Lannuier are displayed in a room from a house built in Richmond, Virginia (Fig. 87). The wainscoting and door and window units are most unusually made of solid mahogany; the woodwork is signed by one "Theo. Nash, Executor," presumably the joiner. Baseboards are of a stone known as King of Prussia marble, quarried only in the Philadelphia area.

Two caryatids support the mantel of the marble fireplace, which is carved with anthemia and other classical motifs. A French gilt-bronze clock (Fig. 86) on the mantel displays a freestanding figure of George Washington (modeled after a portrait by John Trumbull), and patriotic motifs relating to his fame. The other walls are covered with a facsimile of a colorful French scenic wallpaper, a popular embellishment of Federal American homes from New England to Virginia. Made by the Dufour firm of Paris and first published in 1815, the paper celebrates the monuments of Paris. More than a thousand separate silk screens were required to produce the exact copy displayed here. An ornamental plaster rosette in the ceiling is adapted from a design in Asher Benjamin's *American Builder's Companion,* a widely used reference book published at Boston in 1806.

For decades after the Revolution most American households continued to rely upon candles for illumination at nighttime. Good candles were never really inexpensive, and as a matter of domestic economy even such an eminent householder as George Washington kept an account of what it cost him to burn them. In the late eighteenth and early nineteenth centuries glass

Fig. 92. North Family Dwelling, *New Lebanon, New York, 1830–40. The Mount Lebanon community, established in 1785, was the Shakers' spiritual and organizational center. Once described by a visitor "as a place where it is always Sunday," what is left of the Shaker community today is occupied by the Darrow School. This building, torn down in 1973, contained the sisters' retiring room, now in the Museum's collection.*

Fig. 93. Corner of the Shaker Retiring Room, *detail, showing representative objects. The Shakers are famous for oval bentwood boxes of the kind seen here; these are not only lovely to look at but, like all the sect's crafts, beautifully and simply constructed with delicate "fingers" to hold them together. The slat-back chair and the bonnet hung from pegs exemplify the observation of one reporter, who wrote of Shaker interiors that their halls and rooms were "lined with pegs, on which spare chairs, hats, cloaks, bonnets, and shawls are hung." The Shakers themselves explained that they hung "everything but people, and that we leave for the world to do."*
Emily C. Chadbourne Fund, 1972 (1972.187.1–3)

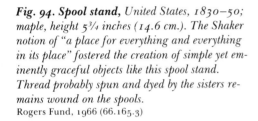

Fig. 94. Spool stand, *United States, 1830–50; maple, height 5¾ inches (14.6 cm.). The Shaker notion of "a place for everything and everything in its place" fostered the creation of simple yet eminently graceful objects like this spool stand. Thread probably spun and dyed by the sisters remains wound on the spools.*
Rogers Fund, 1966 (66.165.3)

94

Fig. 95. Basket, *United States, nineteenth century; wood, wicker, diameter 9¾ inches (24.8 cm.). The New Lebanon Shaker community was apparently a great center of basketmaking. At first made for the use of the brethren, the baskets were eventually produced for sale as the Shakers began to interact with the outside world and the beauty and durability of their products became known. Made from strips of ash especially chosen by experienced Shaker woodsmen, the baskets were woven over molds of many different shapes.*
Rogers Fund, 1966 (66.165.1)

95

93

The Pre–Civil War Period

The Greek Revival, 1820–45

Fig. 96. Gondola chair, workshop of Duncan Phyfe (w. 1792–1847), New York, 1837; mahogany, mahogany veneer, mahogany, ash, height 31 inches (78.7 cm.). Broad, simple curves and plenty of richly grained mahogany give this chair from the Foote suite (see also Fig. 98) its character. The cabinetmaking firm of Joseph Meeks and Sons pictured a very similar chair in their broadside of 1833 (see Fig. 254, No. 12).
Purchase, L. E. Katzenbach Fund Gift, 1966
(66.221.4)

Although the Greek Revival style had precedents in European architecture, it was in America that the fashion struck its deepest roots and won the most popular favor. In the second quarter of the century the landscape from Maine to the farthest western outposts sprouted buildings of every description—city mansions and banks, state capitols and outhouses, modest dwellings, wayside stores and saloons—that in one way or another borrowed forms and ornament from the vocabulary of ancient Greek architecture and expressed them in a native idiom. When Samuel Francis Smith wrote "My Country, 'Tis of Thee" in 1832, he referred to the "templed hills" that were then so characteristic of America's countryside; hills dotted with generally temple-like buildings, many of them made of wood or brick but painted "the whitest of white," as Charles Dickens observed, to suggest gleaming marble.

Books by such leading proponents of the style as Asher Benjamin and Minard Lafever provided models and instructions for city architect and country carpenter alike. Benjamin's works, published at Greenfield, Massachusetts, were widely circulated in numerous editions and had a profound influence on the development of architecture throughout much of New England. Alexander Jackson Davis, a prominent and very versatile architect of the time, designed a number of imposing structures in the Greek Revival style (Fig. 97). Among these were the old New York Customs House (1832–42) on Wall Street (now the Federal Hall National Museum), and Colonnade Row, also known as La Grange Terrace, on Lafayette Street in New York. The latter was originally a continuous row of nine ele-

Fig. 97. Design for a public building, by Alexander Jackson Davis (1803–92), 1835–40; pen and ink, pencil, and watercolor, 12³/₁₆ by 17¹/₂ inches (32.4 by 44.5 cm.). Bold squares and rectangles sparingly ornamented with elements borrowed from Greek temples are characteristic of the Greek Revival style in America. In this design Davis used Doric columns, the plainest of the classical orders, to support a simple triangular pediment. The monumental dignity of the resultant stone facade contrasts strongly with the delicate wood and brick fronts of the earlier Federal style. Much Greek Revival furniture was correspondingly boldly shaped and simply ornamented.
Harris Brisbane Dick Fund, 1924 (24.66.457)

Fig. 98. Greek Revival Parlor. Composed of elements salvaged or copied from Greek Revival houses, this room represents the front parlor of a high-style New York town house of about 1835. The columnar screen with mahogany doors, taken from a New York house, is a particularly fine example of an architectural treatment often found in dwellings with connecting front and back parlors. It is very similar to the design in Plate 60 of Minard Lafever's popular Modern Builder's Guide of 1833. The parlor's expanses of unadorned plaster and mahogany embody the Greek Revival aesthetic and serve as a congenial setting for the parlor suite made in 1837 by Duncan Phyfe for New York lawyer Samuel A. Foote and

his family. The suite contains couches, pier tables, stools, window seats, and side chairs, all with the broad lines and uncarved mahogany surfaces that succeeded the high-relief naturalism of the 1820s. A set of armchairs that descended in Phyfe's family and a drop-front desk in the French manner that is also very likely Phyfe's work complete the furnishings. Upholstery fabric copied from the original Foote suite and a Brussels carpet woven according to a watercolor pattern of 1827 found in the archives of an English carpet mill carry out the Greek Revival theme of bold stylized motifs and strong colors.

Fig. 99. Argand lamp, *labeled "B. Gardiner/N. York," 1835–40; bronze, gilded brass, glass, height 17⅞ inches (45.4 cm.). By using fuel more efficiently than ever before, Argand lamps revolutionized interior lighting. Brighter light and less smoke were its most important features. This example, one of a pair, combines a classical-vase shape and paw feet with flowing acanthus scrolls that foretell the naturalistic curves and foliage of the oncoming rococo style.*
Gift of John C. Cattus, 1967 (67.262.6)

99

100

Fig. 100. Table, *New York, 1830–35; mahogany, mahogany veneer, marble, height 28½ inches (72.4 cm.), diameter 33⅜ inches (84.8 cm.). The broad, plain scrolls that support the handsome black marble top of this center table are echoed by the smaller scrolls that serve as feet. The table's rich marble, mahogany, and gilt surfaces and its pleasing combination of circles and simple scrolls are characteristic of the finest Greek Revival furniture.*
Bertha King Benkard Memorial Fund, 1974 (1974.146)

gant town houses screened by a monumental Corinthian colonnade.

The Museum's Greek Revival room recreates the front parlor of a fashionable New York City town house of about 1835 (Fig. 98). Such a house, built in the 1830s and still standing on West 11th Street, provided the models for the doorways, window casements, and overall proportions of this room. The screen of Ionic columns came from another New York City house of the period, and the black marble fireplace, typical of Greek Revival architecture, was taken from a Rye, New York, house of about 1825. Cornice and ceiling-rosette designs are based on Lafever's *Modern Builder's Guide* of 1833.

Furnishing the room is an Empire parlor suite, thought to have been made by Duncan Phyfe in 1837 for Samuel A. Foote, which illustrates the late, broadly curving Empire fashion at its best. In spite of their heaviness, a pair of méridiennes (daybeds) with asymmetrical backs and arms achieve a monumental grace. Window benches with plain scrolled legs, so-called gondola chairs (Fig. 96), and curule stools are all simple but elegant accompaniments to the daybeds. Crimson linen-and-wool rep upholstery with woven gold medallions, a facsimile of the original fabric, brilliantly sets off the rich color and grain of the mahogany used for these pieces. The plain scrolls and broad uncarved surfaces of the marble-topped center table (Fig. 100) echo those of the Foote suite. Imposing proportions and richly figured mahogany are also distinguishing characteristics of the *secrétaire à abattant* (Fig. 101), which, like the table, is attributed to the shop of Duncan Phyfe.

During this period virtually all the decorative arts made some reference to

Fig. 101. Desk, *attributed to the workshop of Duncan Phyfe (w. 1792–1847), New York, 1825–40; mahogany, mahogany veneers, height 62¼ inches (158.1 cm.). This form, derived from the* secrétaire à abattant *of the French Restauration style, has an upper panel that drops to reveal a luxuriously fitted interior desk section. With its simple rectilinear outlines and its flawless proportions, this desk achieves grandeur through its stunning veneered surface. Except for restrained brass trim where the squared pilasters meet the cornice, no ornament distracts us from the vivid patterns of the veneer. A similar desk, now at the Museum of the City of New York, was made for Governor DeWitt Clinton of New York.* Purchase, The Manney Collection Gift, 1983 (1983.225)

ancient Greek designs. An exceptionally handsome bronze Argand lamp made and labeled by Baldwin Gardiner, a well-known New York retailer, is a case in point (Fig. 99). The oil font is made in the shape of an amphora, the two-handled jar used by Greeks and Romans for carrying oil and wine. The neck is ringed by an egg-and-dart molding in the ancient style. Ormolu paw feet similar to the carved and gilded ones of contemporary furniture emerge from sockets derived from Greek architectural ornament. The lamp was made about 1835 or 1840, and the loose, feathery acanthus scrolls along its oil pipes suggest the rococo styles soon to come into fashion.

101

The Rococo Revival
1840–60

The fading authority of classical styles opened the way for a variety of others, each inspired by a different period of the past. Never in history had there been such a medley of disparate vogues competing for attention, succeeding one another, and often mingling their different designs—a situation that caused confusion which persisted throughout the rest of the nineteenth century. "All we can do," conceded one well-known practitioner, "is to combine, using bits here and there, as our education affords more or less acquaintance with the models from which we steal our material." None of these revival styles was presented without an attribution to a historic style represented by some suggestive element of design—usually employed with imagination and abandon—but these styles tell us more about the nineteenth century than they do about the more distant past.

Fig. 102. The Richard and Gloria Manney, John Henry Belter Rococo Revival Parlor, about 1852. Architectural elements taken from a late Greek Revival house built in Astoria, Queens, New York, in about 1852 are used here in a room that recreates a fashionable mid-1850s parlor such as the one published by Minard Lafever in The Architectural Instructor *(New York, 1856, Pl. LXIII). A set of rosewood furniture by the preeminent New York cabinetmaker and manufacturer John Henry Belter furnishes the parlor. Sets had become popular by the mid-nineteenth century, and one such as this with elaborately carved side and armchairs, sofas, tête-à-têtes, and center and side tables proclaimed the wealth and fashionableness of its owner. The high curving chairbacks are lavishly pierced and carved with characteristically Rococo Revival fruit, flower, and other naturalistic motifs. They are complemented by the richly scrolled carpet, the voluminous and assertively patterned draperies and upholstery, and the gilded, scrolled, and glass-ornamented chandelier.*

102

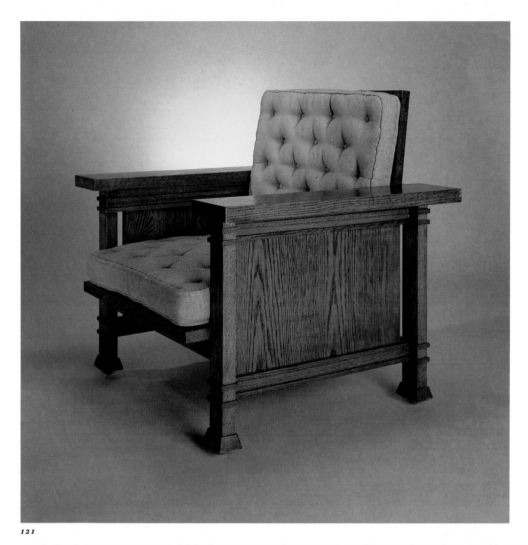

121

Fig. 122. Table, *designed by Frank Lloyd Wright (1867–1959), 1912–14; oak, height 26⁵/₁₆ inches (67.1 cm.). Wright probably designed this library table specifically for this room, and like the other furnishings he designed for the Little house, it is composed of strong horizontals and verticals. The pair of marked bronze candlesticks were designed by Robert Jarvie about 1901 for The Jarvie Shop in Chicago. They were not among the Littles' original furnishings, but are included in the display to illustrate the work of a gifted Arts and Crafts designer to whom Wright gave numerous commissions.*

Purchase, Emily Crane Chadbourne Bequest, 1972 (1972.60.3); Purchase, Mr. and Mrs. David Lubart Gift, in memory of Katherine J. Lubart, 1944–1975, 1981 (1981.157.1,2)

122

FURNITURE

Fig. 123. *Detail, cabinet attributed to the Symonds shops, see Fig. 127.*

The Early Colonial Period 1630–1730

*Figs. 124–29. **Joined furniture,** the most expensive type of the seventeenth century and the most durable, was decorated with carving, painting, and applied ornament. Sometimes only one of these decorative techniques was employed, sometimes two, and sometimes all three. Although only a handful of pieces survive with their original paint, we know that much seventeenth-century furniture was painted. Fortunately, even when the paint has worn off or been removed by an overzealous collector, the carving remains. Motifs were derived from a varied provincial English vocabulary that blended medieval and Renaissance influences. The examples shown here are all shallowly carved, and most show traces of their carvers' scribe lines, made when the designs were being laid out. Flowers and leaves, paired S-scrolls, arches and guilloches (intertwined circles), and geometrical shapes like diamonds and circles are some of the motifs that are often seen. All of these, interpreted and combined differently, may be picked out in the examples shown. The fluid leaves on the Thurston box contrast strongly with the simplified guilloche-and-rosette pattern that ornaments the Buel box, and both are very different from the complicated combination of geometrical and Renaissance-derived motifs of the New Haven Colony chest.*

The forms and designs of seventeenth-century furniture are referred to as Jacobean, after Jacobius, the Latin name for James, because James I reigned in England when the first permanent American settlements were made. The chest was one of the most typical forms of seventeenth-century furniture, as indeed it had been in ages past. In addition to serving as a storage place, it sometimes doubled as a seat, and, since it was portable, as a kind of luggage. Like virtually all case furniture of this early period, chests were uncompromisingly rectangular, constructed of vertical stiles and horizontal rails solidly joined at right angles to frame slightly recessed panels. From the earliest days of settlement, distinctive local and regional differences appeared in the designs applied to this basic form. The front of one example (Fig. 129) is covered with flat carvings that combine late Tudor and Jacobean motifs in the manner associated with William Searle and Thomas Dennis of Ipswich, Massachusetts.

What are commonly referred to as sunflower chests because of the nature of their stylized floral carvings were fashioned exclusively in the Connecticut River valley in the neighborhood of Wethersfield (Fig. 128). These pieces are also decorated with applied split spindles and bosses stained black to simulate ebony. The bosses, reminiscent of generally similar decorations on Elizabethan furniture, are sometimes referred to as "jewels." Still other regional variations in design can be attributed to the furniture makers of such separate centers as Hadley, Salem, Boston, and other New England towns and villages (Figs. 124–27). A point to be made here is that these local differences, so early apparent, were slight but clear indications of the diverse cultural strains that contributed to colonial society and that continued to characterize American craftsmanship in the changing styles of years to come.

The most complex seventeenth-century furniture form was the cupboard—the court cupboard and the press cupboard—used for the display of silver, pewter, brass, and pottery, as well as for storage (see Fig. 13). In America such large and important pieces reached a peak of elaboration late in the century and then quickly went out of fashion, to be replaced by more specialized forms. At the other extreme of size, miniature chests, cabinets, and boxes used for the storage of small objects display essentially the same type of carved and applied ornament that

124

125

126

127

Fig. 127. Cabinet, *attributed to the Symonds shops, Salem, Massachusetts, dated 1679; red oak, white pine, walnut, maple, height 18 inches (45.7 cm.). This diminutive chest, whose center door (see detail, p. 98) conceals ten little drawers for valuables, is a rare form, made for Ephraim and Mary Herrick of Beverly. Like a seventeenth-century child, who was always dressed as a miniature adult, small chests resemble their elders in every detail except size. Applied ornament in the form of pillar-like split spindles flanking an octagonal sunburst formed of moldings and flat triangles, gives a strong architectural effect. Carving is used too, to create the paired S-scrolls that decorate the sides.*
Gift of Mrs. Russell Sage, 1909 (10.125.168)

Fig. 124. Chest, *detail, New Haven Colony, 1640–80; oak, pine. Found in Cheshire, Connecticut.*
Gift of Mrs. George C. Bryant, in memory of her husband, 1947 (47.133.3)

Fig. 125. Box, *attributed to John Thurston (1607–85), Dedham, Massachusetts, 1660–85; oak, pine, height 9½ inches (24.1 cm.).*
Gift of Mrs. Russell Sage, 1909 (10.125.680)

Fig. 126. Box, *attributed to William Buel (here 1630–d. 1681), Windsor, Connecticut, 1640–80; oak, pine, height 9½ inches (24.1 cm.).*
Gift of Mrs. Russell Sage, 1909 (10.125.2)

Fig. 128. Chest with two drawers, *Connecticut, Wethersfield area, 1675–1705; oak, pine, cedar, maple, height 39⅞ inches (101.3 cm.). Chests and cupboards of the so-called sunflower type share panel-and-frame construction with other well-made case pieces of the period, but they combine distinctive low-relief carving with applied moldings and split spindles. Here the usual arrangement of stylized tulips with wavy petals and leaves in the two side panels and "sunflowers"—spiky geometrical Tudor roses—in the center panel is varied, for this example has tulips in all three front panels and the original owner's initials, DC, in the center. Peter Blin of Wethersfield is credited with originating the sunflower form.*
Gift of Mrs. J. Woodhull Overton, 1966 (66.190.1)

Fig. 129. Chest, *Ipswich, Massachusetts, 1660–80; oak, height 29¾ inches (75.6 cm.). In basic form this chest is typical of seventeenth-century colonial work—it is rectangular, made of oak, constructed of panels and frames held together by mortise and tenon joints, and ornamented with motifs taken from geometry, nature, and architecture. But the elaborate combinations of patterns that decorate the facade and its deep, rich carving place the chest in a small, celebrated group of objects attributed to William Searle (1634–67) and Thomas Dennis (1638–1706), both of whom were trained in Devonshire, England, came to America, and worked in Ipswich. The strong rectangular outline of the chest is balanced and softened by the rounded forms of much of its ornament.*
Gift of Mrs. Russell Sage, 1909 (10.125.685)

128

129

130

131

appears on larger pieces (Fig. 127).

The collection also includes one of the earliest known American tables, consisting of trestles supporting a removable board that could be put aside to clear space when the table wasn't in use, and an oaken table tightly joined in a boxlike form with turned legs and a skirt molded and underlined by a decorative edging (Figs. 130 and 131).

The progression of styles from the last decades of the seventeenth century through the first decades of the eighteenth, and the influences that conditioned their design, are succinctly summarized in seating furniture. Seventeenth-century chairs made few concessions to comfort and even the frequent addition of loose cushions provided little respite. These straight-lined, firm, and often elaborately turned and carved chairs did however impose upon the sitter a measure of dignity and importance. (At a time when tables often consisted of removable boards set upon trestles, he who occupied the principal seat had the distinction we recall in the phrase "chairman of the board.")

Among examples that illustrate these points is a chair that is today sometimes called a Brewster chair because Elder William Brewster (d. 1644) of Plymouth Plantation is said to have owned one of this type (Fig. 132). With its eight banks of turned spindles and its massive posts, this very rare survival from the seventeenth century is one of the most venerable relics in early American furniture.

One of the earliest and grandest types of seating furniture made in colonial America is the wainscot chair (Fig. 133). Characterized by a solid wooden back and seat and an almost formidably solid basic structure, chairs of this kind were

146

Fig. 146. Slate tabletop, *Switzerland, about 1720; slate and inlay of various European woods, length 35⅛ inches (89.2 cm.). Most furniture used in colonial America was made here, although occasionally English pieces were imported, so it is unusual and interesting to come across a small group of slate-topped tables whose bases were made in America, but whose elaborate slate-and-inlaid-wood tops seem to have come from Switzerland. It has been suggested that the tabletops were imported as a group by some enterprising merchant, to whom they were shipped via the Rhine to Rotterdam and then to New England.*
The Sylmaris Collection, Gift of George Coe Graves, 1930 (30.120.56)

147

Fig. 147. William and Mary furniture *ranging from very special to standard for the eighteenth century is shown in the Metcalf Bowler Room. The walnut gateleg table, a space-saving form that became popular in this period, was made in New England between 1700 and 1730. It is surrounded by several rush-bottomed chairs that combine William and Mary bases with Queen Anne backs—a type that was made in large numbers throughout the middle years of the eighteenth century, and very possibly later. To the right is an elaborate Gaines version of the standard rush-bottomed chairs across the table (see Fig. 144), and in the background is a leather chair of the Boston variety. Next to it is a slate-topped table, a rare form in America. Nowadays*

sometimes called a mixing table because its slate top permitted mixing drinks without worrying about spills, this form consisted of a base with trumpet-turned legs and arched skirt like that of a dressing table and a slate-and-inlaid-wood top imported from Switzerland (see Fig. 146).
Rogers Fund, 1916 (16.120)

The Late Colonial Period, 1730–90

Fig. 148. Armchair, *Philadelphia, 1740–60; walnut, height 41 inches (104.1 cm). Much of the richest Queen Anne and Chippendale furniture made in the colonies comes from Philadelphia, which by 1750 had become, after London, the most prosperous city in the English-speaking world. Prosperity and sophistication are reflected in the suave curves of this armchair—in its generously scrolled splat, inviting outward-curved armrests, and cabriole legs ending in dainty slipper feet. Its rear legs are the stumplike posts characteristic of Philadelphia seating furniture.* Rogers Fund, 1925 (25.115.36)

148

The late colonial interiors and furniture that superseded those of the William and Mary period date largely from the middle decades of the eighteenth century, a period culminating in the Revolutionary War. The increasing use of mahogany along with handsomely grained black walnut made for more opulent appearances.

With the introduction of the Queen Anne style in furniture every trace of Tudor and Puritan stiffness vanished. The elaborate ornamental scrolls, turnings, and pierced carvings of high-style William and Mary furniture gave way to undulating curved elements that both please the eye and serve the needs of solid comfort. Decorative carving played only a secondary role in this suave harmony of form and function. In 1712 Lord Shaftsbury rationalized this newly conceived simplicity and unity in design: "In short we are to carry this remembrance still along with us," he wrote, "that the fewer the objects are besides those that are absolutely necessary in a piece, the easier it is for the eye by one simple act, and in one view to comprehend the sum or whole."

The single most conspicuous element of this graceful construction was the cabriole leg, a reverse-curved support with a shaped foot (Fig. 148). The term cabriole comes from the Italian *capriola,* goat's leap, and the form itself from a type of support derived in ancient times from the profile of an animal's hind leg. Curves were often repeated in serpentine stretchers, horseshoe-shaped seats, and solid vase-shaped splats molded to the contours of the human spine and framed by rounded supporting stiles continuous with arched crest rails. Colonial furniture makers first employed the cabriole leg about 1730. Boston,

Newport, New York, and Philadelphia—as well as other regions—each had its own distinctive interpretation of the style. Chairs made in Philadelphia during the middle years of the century, some departing into Chippendale flourishes, reached a peak of sophistication.

The basic elements of style of any period are probably more immediately visible in a piece of seating furniture than in any other form. The transition from earlier fashions was often gradual, however, and elements of a fading style may be combined with those of one on the rise. An extremely rare walnut settee in the Wing has a tall back whose curved outlines recall chair backs of the late seventeenth century (Fig. 149). On the other hand, its cabriole legs with shell carvings on the knees announce the newer style of the Queen Anne period. (The legs terminate in trifid feet, a re-finement often adopted by Philadelphia furniture makers.) This exceptional piece descended in the family of James Logan, at one time William Penn's secretary and the builder of Stenton, a handsome country seat that still stands near Germantown, Pennsylvania. Logan, a scholar and a botanist as well as a statesman, had amassed a fortune in land investments and in trade with the Indians. He was so content to remain in his suburban retreat that he retired from public service to enjoy life there.

Generally speaking, lean proportions and restrained ornamentation are regional characteristics of furniture made in New England (Fig. 150). The relatively slender legs and narrow backs of chairs are typical features of this form in both the Queen Anne and Chippendale styles. An easy chair in the Queen Anne style retains its original uphol-

Fig. 149. Settee, *Philadelphia, 1740–60; walnut, yellow pine, height 48 inches (121.9 cm). A few sofas and settees were made as early as the William and Mary period, and during the Queen Anne and Chippendale eras they gradually replaced their predecessor, the daybed, but the form was not frequently made until the Federal period. This rare early settee gracefully unites William and Mary and Queen Anne design with its high, boldly scrolled back and shell-carved cabriole legs and trifid feet (the latter characteristic of only the finest Philadelphia Queen Anne furniture). It descended in the family of James Logan, scholar, statesman, merchant, onetime secretary and lifelong friend to William Penn. It is both the earliest known American settee and the only known Philadelphia example in the Queen Anne style.* Rogers Fund, 1925 (25.115.1)

149

Fig. 150. Side chair, *Connecticut, 1740–70; maple, painted, height 43¼ inches (109.9 cm.). One of a set of four in the Museum's collection, this chair belongs to a group that has recently been associated with the Lothrops, cabinetmakers of Norwich and Wallingford, Connecticut. A set of similar chairs descended in the Lothrop family, and the needlework seat on a similar example in the collection of the Henry Ford Museum is signed by one of the Lothrop girls, so since many of the Lothrops were joiners, an attribution to their shops seems justified. Although simplicity and restraint are characteristic of New England chairs in general, Connecticut examples are often straighter and stiffer than chairs from neighboring colonies. The pinched splat, straight stiles, and high shoulders seen here are characteristic of Connecticut, as is the square seat.*
Gift of Mrs. J. Insley Blair, 1946 (46.194.1)

Fig. 151. Crewel-embroidered linen chair seat, *perhaps by a member of the Lothrop family of Norwich and Wallingford, Connecticut, detail of Fig. 150. Any chair that retains its original fabric covering is a rarity, and if the decoration of that covering is as fresh and charming as this crewelwork scene, it is a great bonus. The placid lion and the frisky dog and the deer in this crewelwork scene gambol in a landscape stitched in red, blue, yellow, and green. The other three chairs in this group have equally engaging, but different, crewelwork seats.*
Gift of Mrs. J. Insley Blair, 1946 (46.194.1)

151

stery, the front and sides covered with finely worked needlepoint and the back with a colorful landscape worked in crewel (Figs. 153 and 154). The chair is unique in being signed and dated by the upholsterer, "Gardner Junr" (Fig. 152).

The cabriole curve that transformed Queen Anne chairs lent the same grace to tables of the period, and examples from New England have a delicacy that sets them apart from tables of other regions (Fig. 155). Case furniture is more dainty, too. A mahogany spinet supported by four cabriole legs with pad feet in the Queen Anne style is the earliest American work by an immigrant member of a family of eminent London musical-instrument makers (Fig. 157). A panel above the keyboard of this exceptional piece bears the inscription "John Harris Boston New England fecit." When it was completed in 1769 and shipped off to a Newport customer (probably to the merchant Francis Malbone, in whose family it subsequently descended) the Boston press daily and proudly reported that this "very curious Spinnet" was "the first ever made in America." Actually this distinction belongs to another spinet in the Museum's collection, made thirty years earlier by Johann Clemm of Philadelphia.

A walnut-veneered and inlaid high-

150

dition of lavish rococo carving. Perhaps the richest and most beautifully proportioned of all such pieces is this, known as the Pompadour high chest because its carved female bust reminded some romantic early collector of Louis XV's mistress. The design for urn finials on either side of the central bust is a modified version of a design taken from Chippendale's The Gentleman and Cabinet-Maker's Director, *while the design of the central bottom drawer is taken, again with some modification, from another pattern book of the period, Thomas Johnson's* New Book of Ornament. *Finials and drawer, as well as all other carved ornament on this splendid piece, are of the highest order and were very possibly executed by English craftsmen who had immigrated to Philadelphia. A nineteenth-century chronicler reported that towering chests of drawers like this were often found in eighteenth-century parlors or sitting rooms, and, he added, "It was no sin to rummage them before company!"*
John Stewart Kennedy Fund, 1918 (18.110.4)

188

Fig. 188. Side chair, *Philadelphia, about 1770; mahogany, southern white cedar, height 37 inches (94 cm.). Chairs of this degree of richness are extremely rare in American work, and for many years such a piece would have been identified either as simply "English," or as a member of a group of "sample chairs" attributed to Benjamin Randolph. Lately, however, these chairs (so far six others from this set have come to light) and a card table with similar carving have been attributed to Thomas Affleck, like Randolph an outstanding Philadelphia craftsman. The chairs, table, and a number of other pieces were apparently ordered between 1770 and 1772 by General John Cadwalader, leading citizen and fervent patriot, for his elegant town house in Philadelphia. The lavishly scalloped skirt, hairy-paw feet, and wide saddle seat are much more English in feeling than American, but the stump rear legs and the construction techniques, as well as the flowing naturalistic carving, bespeak a Philadelphia origin. Because of the richness and rarity of this set, one of these chairs recently established a world auction record in New York.*
Purchase, Sansbury-Mills and Rogers Funds, Emily C. Chadbourne Gift, Virginia Groomes Gift, in memory of Mary W. Groomes, Mr. and Mrs. Marshall P. Blankarn, John Bierwirth and Robert G. Goelet Gifts, The Sylmaris Collection, Gift of George Coe Graves, by exchange, and funds from various donors, 1974 (1974.325)

Fig. 189. Pembroke table, *Philadelphia, 1765–90; mahogany, oak, white pine, height 28 inches (71.1 cm.). The Pembroke, or breakfast, table was a new form in the Chippendale period and was named, according to Sheraton in his* Cabinet Dictionary *of 1803, for the lady who first ordered one. These useful small tables reverse the proportions of the earlier drop leaf, making the midsection wider than the leaves. This example is one of the finest of its type, but it relies for its effect on overall form and proportion instead of on the lush carving that gives so much Philadelphia Chippendale furniture its character. The curves of the scalloped leaves are repeated in the rising crossed stretchers; both provide a contrast to the straight, square-sectioned Marlborough legs.*
Purchase, Emily C. Chadbourne Gift, 1974 (1974.35)

189

Fig. 190. Group of Pennsylvania German furnishings in the Pennsylvania German room from Morgantown, Lancaster County, about 1761. Simple, useful forms that would have served well in a bustling Pennsylvania German household are gathered here. The unpainted tables and open-shelved dresser are of walnut, a wood often used in Pennsylvania furniture even during the Chippendale period, when mahogany had become the fashionable wood. The corner fireplace retains its original blue paint, now much faded, and its overmantel painting—a rather grim scene with crosses marking wayside graves, copied from an English book on drawing and engraving. Pewter and woodenware dishes, as well as brightly decorated (and today much col-lected) slip- and sgraffito wares, indicate what would have appeared on a typical eighteenth-century Pennsylvania German table.
Chimney breast and chair rail: Morris K. Jesup Fund, 1934 (34.27.1,10)

Fig. 191. Dower chest, Berks County, Pennsylvania, about 1780; yellow pine, painted, tulip poplar, height 28⅝ inches (72.7 cm.). In Pennsylvania German country, painted-pine furniture was the alternative to the type seen in Fig. 190. Traditional German construction and decorative techniques were used, but the influence of the English who had first settled Pennsylvania is seen in the choice of motifs. The unicorns in the center were copied from the unicorn on the British coat of arms, while the horsemen with raised swords in the two side panels are English cavalry officers. The batwing brasses on the two lower drawers are English, too. In joining influences from both German and English cultures, Pennsylvania German furniture was a joyful and unique expression of the environment of the new land.
Rogers Fund, 1923 (23.16)

190

Fig. 210. Mantel, *carving by Samuel McIntire (active about 1782–1811), Salem, about 1795; wood, composition, height 54¾ inches (139.1 cm.), length 77 inches (195.6 cm.). When Elias Hasket and Elizabeth Derby's mansion was torn down in 1815, the eminent clergyman and diarist William Bentley lamented that "It was the best finished, most elegant, and best constructed House I ever saw. . . . The heirs could not agree to occupy it and the convenience of the spot for other buildings bought a sentence of destruction for it. . . ." After it was taken down many of its elegant architectural elements were advertised in the Salem* Gazette, *including "8 richly ornamented Chimney Pieces," of which this is believed to be the only survivor. It was not the most magnificent mantel in this very grand house, however, for the advertisement also offered "2 marble Chimney Pieces, one very elegant." The ornament here is of composition (a plaster-like substance that could be molded into very delicate shapes) except for that on the columns, which McIntire is said to have carved. Garlands composed of the grape bunches and leaves associated with the master's work spiral down each column.*
Rogers Fund, 1946 (46.76)

Fig. 211. Oval-backed side chair, *Philadelphia, 1796 or 1801; maple painted dark brown with polychrome decoration, white pine, height 38½ inches (97.8 cm.). This charmingly painted chair is thought to be one of the twenty-four that Elias Hasket Derby ordered for his magnificent new house in Salem. Others thought to be part of Derby's order have the same oval back enclosing a beribboned bouquet of feathers but are painted white instead of blackish brown. Possibly their maker-decorator had recently come to America from England, where similar chairs had been produced by the prestigious London firm of Gillow before Hepplewhite published his version of the design in 1788.*
Gift of Mrs. J. Insley Blair, 1947 (47.103.1)

211

Fig. 212. Sideboard, attributed to the workshop of Thomas Seymour (active 1794–1843), Boston, 1805–15; mahogany and birch veneers; birch, cherry, and holly inlays; white pine and cherry; length 73 inches (185.4 cm.). The sideboard was a new form in the Federal period—one so useful that it became popular immediately. Each prosperous center produced a characteristic version, and this example represents Boston cabinetmaking at its best. Its beautifully matched veneers, each set off by light-wood banding; tambour section with flat alternating light and dark strips; turned and carved legs; and delicate inlaid ivory urns that serve as keyhole escutcheons (see also Fig. 221) are some of the many elegant details that contribute to the very high quality of this sideboard. The Seymours, who are believed to have made it, were Boston's outstanding furniture makers in this period, producing pieces comparable in quality and stylishness to those Duncan Phyfe was turning out in New York.
Gift of the family of Mr. and Mrs. Andrew Varick Stout, in their memory, 1965 (65.188.1)

212

Fig. 213. Worktable, attributed to Lemuel Churchill (active 1805–about 1828), carving attributed to Thomas Whitman (active 1809), Boston, 1810–15; mahogany veneer, mahogany, brass stringing, ebony turnings, ivory inlay, mahogany, tulip poplar, height 28⅝ inches (72.7 cm.). The worktable was newly created in the Federal period to provide convenient storage and work space for sedentary activities like sewing, reading, and writing. This example has the rounded outlines of the later, archeologically oriented neoclassical period. Its lyre-shaped pedestal, curved legs with brass paw feet, and segmentally reeded ovolo corners are all features of the oncoming Empire style, taken in this case from English designs of the Regency period. Lemuel Churchill, to whom the table is attributed because the name "Churchill" is scrawled on its underside, was also the maker of a labeled lolling chair that is now in the Winterthur Museum collection.
Gift of Solomon Grossman, 1980 (1980.508)

213

Fig. 214. Tambour desk, labeled by Reuben Swift (active 1802–early 1820s), New Bedford, Massachusetts, about 1805; mahogany, burl walnut; flame-grain birch, tulip, and maple veneers; white pine, birch; height 55 inches (139.7 cm.). It was not until Reuben Swift's tour de force surfaced a few years ago that we had any inkling of the production of such fashionable furniture in New Bedford. So far, this is the only labeled piece by Swift to come to light, and the only piece of such magnificence to have a documented New Bedford history. This desk, made about 1805, was the most fashionable type of desk made in New England during the Federal period except for the much larger breakfront; its tambour closing, a newly fashionable feature, and its brilliant contrasting veneers, are characteristic of New England. It is unusual, however, in substituting a full case of drawers beneath the desk section, for most tambour desks have only one or two long shallow drawers. Swift's use of dazzling veneers is unexpected as well. An unusually refined detail is the diaper design executed in marquetry on the two top drawers.
Bequest of Cecile L. Mayer, 1962 (62.171.6)

Up in Salem, Massachusetts, woodworkers were deriving inspiration from English design books too. A Salem-made chair carved by the ingenious Samuel McIntire, for example, is lifted from a plate in Hepplewhite's *Guide* practically without a change (Figs. 208 and 209). Such literal copying was not the rule, however. More frequently, cabinetmakers merged the elements suggested by design books so variously that the result is most aptly referred to simply as being in the Federal style.

Samuel McIntire was one of the most prominent and versatile of the artisans who worked in the Federal style, a superb craftsman who applied his skills to ships and buildings as well as to furniture. Like other fine woodworkers of his own and earlier times he also mended fences and built pigsties, and he may have made such commonplace necessities as washtubs and ironing boards. However, he was primarily an accomplished architect, designer, and carver—and a competent musician. When he died in 1811, an obituary affectionately characterized him as "one of the best of men." Thanks largely to his art and industry Salem became the handsomest New England town of the late eighteenth century.

The carved eagle and swags, raised elements set against a stippled background on a Sheraton "Square Sofa" (Figs. 206 and 207), are in McIntire's individual style. His gifts as an architect enabled him to design, on an entirely different scale, the house of Elias Hasket Derby, an adventurous and successful shipowner who became New England's first millionaire. The Derby residence was "more like a palace than the dwelling of an American merchant," according to a visitor from Baltimore. McIntire personally worked on many of the details that distinguished that celebrated but short-lived structure (it was demolished in 1815 and its furnishings dispersed). Apparently all that remains of the mansion is a mantelpiece ornamented with classical scenes and motifs, preserved in the Museum (Fig. 210). Fortunately, other Salem houses built by McIntire still stand in testimony to the man's architectural skills. The Peirce-Nichols and Pingree houses, one of frame construction and the other of brick, are among the outstanding Federal residences.

214

215

Fig. 215. Lolling chair, *Massachusetts, 1790–1800; mahogany, birch, height 44½ inches (113 cm.). Made almost exclusively in New England, the lolling chair (sometimes also called the Martha Washington chair) is a descendant of earlier French and English open-arm chairs with upholstered back and seat. Joseph Nichol Scott's* A New Universal Dictionary *of 1764 defines "to loll" as "To lean lazily against, or lie idly upon any thing"—a definition that conjures up a picture of an elegant gentleman lounging in such a chair. The term is contemporary with the chairs, for it turns up in advertisements and inventories. This example exhibits the high back with serpentine crest that is characteristic of many Massachusetts lolling chairs. The serpentine curve is repeated in the line of the arms, which are skillfully fashioned with a hollow for the elbow to rest in.*
Bequest of Flora E. Whiting, 1971 (1971.180.15)

Figs. 216–26. *Furniture and architectural details* from the Museum's collection illustrate, on the left-hand page, the early Federal taste for flat surfaces with symmetrically disposed ornament. Motifs were idealized or stylized, like the églomisé, inlaid, painted, and carved classical and naturalistic forms illustrated here. By the

end of the first decade of the nineteenth century, delicacy was giving way to the highly sculptural carved ornament of the later Federal period. Now the trend was toward high-relief renderings of naturalistic motifs like the swan, paw feet, and the eagle atop a rock pile seen on the right-hand page. Paint was still fashionable, but colors grew

deeper and richer, and gilding was frequently lavishly applied to create the boldly assertive forms of the 1810s and 1820s.

Eglomisé *panel, desk and bookcase:* Gift of Mrs. Russell Sage and various other donors, 1969 (69.203); *shell inlay, gentleman's secretary:* Joseph Pulitzer Bequest, 1967 (67.203); *painted feather detail, side chair:* Gift of Mrs. J. Insley Blair, 1947 (47.103.1); *carved feather detail,*

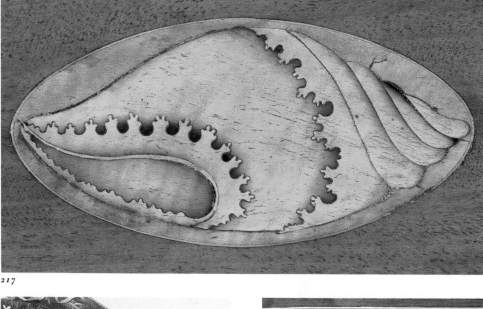

217

216

218

219

220

221

square-back side chair: Gift of the Members of the Committee of the Bertha King Benkard Memorial Fund, 1946 (46.67.102); *urn finial, gentleman's secretary:* Purchase, Gift of Mrs. Russell Sage, Bequest of Ethel Yocum, Bequest of Charlotte E. Hoadley, and Rogers Fund, by exchange, 1971 (1971.9); *inlaid urn, sideboard:* Gift of the family of Mr. and Mrs. Andrew Varick Stout, in their memory, 1965 (65.188.1); *swan support, pier table:* Friends of the American Wing Fund,

1968 (68.43); *carved paw foot, Phyfe pier table:* Gift of John C. Cattus, 1967 (67.262.2); *carved and gilded paw foot, Lannuier pier table:* Rogers Fund, 1953 (53.181); *marble fireplace detail:* Gift of Joe Kindig, Jr., 1968 (68.137); *carved and gilded eagle crest, girandole mirror:* Rogers Fund, 1921 (21.44.2)

222

223

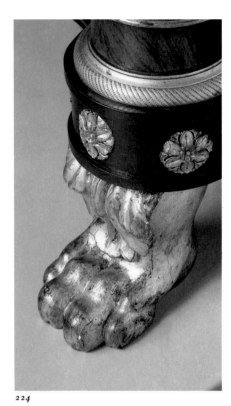

224

225

226

227

Fig. 227. *View of the Federal Gallery showing a pillar-and-claw dining table attributed to the workshop of Duncan Phyfe, a set of lyre-back chairs by Phyfe, and a pair of marble-topped pier tables perhaps also made in Phyfe's workshop. Although the parlor was still the most elegant room in the house, the dining room was becoming a close second and required the creation of specialized pieces like these. Instead of the flashing veneers of New England and the Middle Colonies, Phyfe favored solid mahogany ornamented with low-relief carving of stylized motifs taken from the classical vocabulary. Characteristic examples are paw feet, hairy shanks, lyres, and ribbons of waterleaves—all of which may be seen here.*

Fig. 228. Side chair, *made by Duncan Phyfe (w. 1792–1847), New York, 1810–20; mahogany, height 32¼ inches (82.6 cm.). Delicate klismos chairs of this type represent a transition from Phyfe's earliest chairs with round, reeded legs and square backs to the more fully archeological curule chairs (see Figs. 87 and 89). Here we have an ancient shape—the curving klismos with both front and back legs sweeping away from the chair in an arc—and details found on ancient furniture, such as dog's-paw feet with hairy shanks and lyre splat, but the proportions are still those of the early Federal period, and the whole is executed with a very light touch. This is one of a set of chairs Phyfe made for the family of New Jersey governor William Livingston. The Museum's collection contains thirteen of the original set of twenty-four (see Fig. 227).*
Gift of the family of Mr. and Mrs. Andrew Varick Stout, in their memory, 1965 (65.188.2)

A pair of exceptional painted chairs with open oval backs framing six curved plumes and other decorative motifs, generally patterned after a design in Hepplewhite's *Guide*, were probably made in Philadelphia for a member of the prominent Derby family of Salem (Fig. 211). It is certain, at least, that in 1796 Elias Hasket Derby ordered two dozen chairs of similar design from Philadelphia, and these could have been part of that shipment.

A sideboard that was probably made in the workshop of Thomas Seymour of Boston offers an individualistic variation of the Sheraton style (Fig. 212). Sideboards were introduced to America during the Federal period, as dining rooms assumed an increasingly important role in social life. In the words of Robert Adam, they had become "apartments of conversation." (Some English sideboards, and probably some American ones, were supplied with a small cupboard containing a chamber pot for the immediate relief of those who drank too much during the course of a long, drawn-out, possibly garrulous dinner party.) Seymour was an English immigrant, but the American work attributed to him speaks with a decidedly personal, New England accent. Another elegant Boston piece is a worktable attributed to Lemuel Churchill (Fig. 213). This form was new in the Federal period, and is another indication of that era's growing interest in specialized objects for specific functions—in this case that of holding a lady's sewing and writing equipment.

Until a few years ago when the Museum acquired a desk bearing his label (Fig. 214), the name of Reuben Swift of New Bedford had been all but forgotten. An original and sophisticated interpretation of prevailing styles with, among other highly refined details, tambour closings and richly contrasting woods in plain and marquetry surfaces, this piece alone is enough to establish Swift as a cabinetmaker of imagination and rare competence.

One of the most graceful and distinctively American chairs ever made, with a high upholstered back and open arms, was known to contemporaries as a "lolling" chair; sometimes in this country, for no known reason, it was called a Martha Washington chair (Fig. 215). This example was made in Massachu-

Figs. 233–37. Shelf and wall clocks. *Time-pieces were expensive and scarce in America until mass-produced clocks were developed in the nineteenth century. New types that were somewhat less expensive than the traditional, or "grandfather," clocks had begun to appear in the second half of the eighteenth century, however. These were shelf and wall clocks, which were cheaper because less brass was required for their works than for a tall clock and because their cases were much smaller and therefore less expensive to make. One of the first was the Massachusetts shelf clock, developed by Aaron Willard, one of the renowned clockmaking Willard brothers, but also produced by a number of other Massachusetts makers. The example shown here (Fig. 233), by David Wood, represents the type at its finest. The banjo clock (Fig. 234) was the invention of another Willard brother, Simon, and it, too, was made by many other clockmakers. Another of Simon Willard's apparently original inventions is the "Eddystone Lighthouse Alarm Time Piece," patented in 1822 (Fig. 235). The works of this unusual form didn't function very well, however, and production was soon discontinued. By about 1816 Eli*

Terry of Connecticut had developed simple wooden works whose parts could be mass produced and housed in the popular pillar-and-scroll case. Like the Willards before him, Terry found that other makers quickly picked up his ideas and produced similar clocks. The pillar-and-scroll example shown here is by Seth Thomas (Fig. 236). A later development produced the "acorn" clock, in which tightly coiled springs replaced the weights of previous examples. The top of its case is shaped like an acorn and is flanked by two acorn finials (Fig. 237). The painted decoration of the lower section shows a sailboat drifting by a Gothic Revival house of about the same period as the clock itself.

Fig. 233. *Shelf clock, works by David Wood (active 1792–1824), Newburyport, Massachusetts, 1792–1800; mahogany, mahogany veneer, white pine, height 27¾ inches (70.5 cm.).*
The Sylmaris Collection, Gift of George Coe Graves, 1930 (30.120.53)

Fig. 234. *Wall (banjo) clock, Massachusetts, 1815–25; mahogany, gilt gesso, églomisé tablets, white pine, tulip poplar, height 43 inches (109.2 cm.).*
Bequest of William B. Whitney, 1937 (37.37.3)

Fig. 235. *"Eddystone Lighthouse Alarm Time Piece," works by Simon Willard (active 1766–1839), Roxbury, Massachusetts, 1825–30; mahogany, mahogany veneer on white pine, white pine, height 28½ inches (72.4 cm.).*
Gift of Mrs. Richard M. Lederer, in memory of her husband, 1957 (57.57)

Fig. 236. *Shelf clock, pillar-and-scroll type, works by Seth Thomas (active about 1806–59), Plymouth, Connecticut, 1820; mahogany, mahogany and maple veneers, white pine, height 27⅞ inches (70.8 cm.).*
Rogers Fund, 1962 (62.195)

Fig. 237. *Shelf clock, "acorn" type, by the Forestville Clock Manufactory, Bristol, Connecticut, 1847–50; rosewood laminated to pine, height 24⅜ inches (61.9 cm.).*
Gift of Mrs. Paul Moore, 1970 (1970.289.6)

236

237

The Shaker Vernacular

Fig. 238. Double counter, *New Lebanon, New York, about 1825; pine, length 68 inches (172.7 cm.). This convenient combination of chest of drawers and table was originally used in the sisters' weaving room at New Lebanon. The Shaker commitment to a life of honesty and purity led to their making objects that were simple, sturdy, and unassumingly graceful. Plain pine finished only with a light coat of red paint, simple moldings and turned knobs, and the utterly serviceable rectangular shape of this counter are characteristic of Shaker humility and practicality.*
Friends of the American Wing Fund, 1966 (66.10.14)

Fig. 239. Sewing table, *stamped "Jas. X. Smith, New-Lebanon, N. Y." and "1843"; cherry, butternut, pine, height 28 inches (71.1 cm.). Shaker furniture, household utensils, and gadgets often included ingenious features that made their user's task easier and smoother. This sewing table, for example, combines a case of drawers, an ample sewing surface, and a yardstick—which is marked off on the front edge of the top. Like the double counter, this table eschews all ornament in favor of straight lines, natural finish, and unobtrusive turned wooden knobs, one to a drawer. Brasses and escutcheons were never used on Shaker furniture—they were unnecessary ornament and therefore unacceptable.*
Friends of the American Wing Fund, 1966 (66.10.18)

238

239

For almost a century following the American Revolution the various Shaker communities scattered about the countryside were building structures and creating artifacts of unique character and quality. While successive generations of non-Shaker architects, craftsmen, and manufacturers worked to keep abreast of ever-changing fashions, Shaker craftsmen motivated by religious ardor unalterably dedicated their hearts and hands to the production of useful objects stripped of all pretense to formal style. The utter simplicity of their designs and the unhurried, meticulous workmanship by which they were realized resulted in functional objects of singular and delicate grace.

The first small contingent of Shakers, led by "Mother Ann" Lee, came to America from England just before the outbreak of the Revolution and eventually settled at Watervliet, New York. Mother Ann was an illiterate, slum-born millworker who had been imprisoned in England because of her zealous preachments against prevailing social mores. But she was an inspired leader. Among her homely injunctions were "Put your hands to work and your hearts to God" and "Do your work as though you had a thousand years to live, and as if you were to die tomorrow." Her followers grew in number with the passing years, as did the communal Shaker societies. An outgrowth of the Quakers, the Shakers were so named because they expressed their religious enthusiasms in agitated dancing, marching, and singing.

By 1840 some thirty Shaker colonies had been established from Maine to Indiana. The sect had reexamined the problems and responsibilities of men and women who must live together in a human association and had eliminated from their lives all that they considered unnecessary. They were frugal, industrious, and celibate. Their typical garb was utterly plain and completely unfashionable. Their austere concept of what made for a good life on earth (with heavenly rewards) was reflected in everything they produced. For them, to labor faithfully, painstakingly, and diligently was akin to praying. As one student of their craftsmanship has observed, Shaker furniture was religion in wood. Indeed they believed, wrote one visitor to the Watervliet community, that the furniture they made was originally designed in heaven (Figs. 238–40).

240

Windsors

Shaker furniture designs and practices were rooted in the vernacular of eighteenth-century America, as the swivel chair with Windsor-like back, an innovation developed in certain Shaker communities in the third quarter of the nineteenth century (Fig. 240), makes clear. Of all forms of vernacular furniture made in America, the Windsor chair was probably the most conspicuous example (Fig. 241). Obviously related to English models of the same general sort, such "stick" furniture assumed a special—and especially graceful—character as it was developed in this country. In its various regional interpretations it departed sharply from any of the fashionable designs of successive periods. No other type of furniture made in America enjoyed such wide and enduring popularity in all ranks of society. George Washington used Windsors on his Mount Vernon porch, Benjamin Franklin had them in his Philadelphia home, Thomas Jefferson ordered four dozen of them for Monticello, and members of the Continental Congress sat in Windsors as they deliberated the cause of American independence. Over the years large quantities of them were shipped to various parts of the world.

One wit has observed that these light, inexpensive, durable, and highly functional forms had "an infinite capacity for taking strains." Adaptations of Windsor principles of construction persisted over many years, and variations of the form are still being made.

Fig. 241. Windsor writing-arm chair, United States, eighteenth century; wood, painted, height 46⁹⁄₁₆ inches (118.2 cm.), depth at writing arm 32 inches (81.3 cm.). By the period of the American Revolution the most popular inexpensive all-purpose chair was the Windsor. Although its antecedents were European, the American Windsor evolved in its own distinctive way. Simply constructed of spindles stuck into a plank seat, it was lightweight, strong, and cheap. Because Windsors were easily movable, they were especially popular for use in the garden, on the porch, and in the hall, as well as for public rooms, but they could be useful anywhere in the house, be it rich or poor. Different kinds of wood with different properties were used for each part of the chair, which was then painted to unify the various wood grains and colors and to provide a protective coating. Combining a writing surface and storage space for reading and writing implements with a Windsor armchair resulted in the eminently practical, but today very rare, form seen here—a compact, movable desk and chair. Gift of Mrs. Screven Lorillard, 1952 (52.195.11)

241

Folk Art

There never has been a time when American furniture has not been painted either in plain colors or in decorative designs of various kinds. Painting inexpensive wood with graining to simulate costly materials was common practice from an early date. So, too, was the more or less elaborate ornamentation of flat surfaces with pictorial subjects of one sort or another—traditional folk themes, peopled landscapes, purely decorative patterns, and the like. The painted furniture of the Pennsylvania Germans offers conspicuous examples, standing distinctly apart from the other early decorated forms in the collection of the Wing (see Fig. 191).

The dividing line between what might most properly be called folk furniture and other forms, traditional and sometimes innovative, cannot always be sharply drawn, but there should be no question about these two bold, ingenuous pieces (Figs. 242 and 243).

Fig. 242. Chest, *attributed to Nehemiah Randall (1770–1850), Belchertown, Massachusetts, 1800–20; pine, painted, length 37³/₄ inches (95.9 cm.). The maker of this lively chest would seem to have trained as a carpenter rather than a cabinetmaker, for the motifs he chose belong to the house-builder's repertoire. The fluted central oval and the borders of painted dentils and rosettes may be seen on mantelpieces, overdoors, and cornices of Federal-period houses. The oval and the arches that originally finished the skirt were laid out with a compass and ruler.*
Gift of Mrs. E. Herrick Low, Nelson Holland and Hudson Holland, in memory of their mother, Mrs. Nelson Clarke Holland, 1955 (55.84)

242

Fig. 243. Table, *New York State, about 1800; pine, painted, height 29¹/₂ inches (74.9 cm.). The maker of this stand used paint to simulate lively wavy and scalloped inlay on the two drawers and varicolored stringing on the legs. Although his stiff cabriole legs ending in squared-off shod feet and overhanging top with scalloped corners indicate a reluctance to give up elements of the previous Chippendale style, the simulated inlay and bail drawer handles are characteristic of the Federal period.*
Purchase, Virginia Groomes Gift, in memory of Mary W. Groomes, and funds from various donors, 1976 (1976.175)

243

The Pre–Civil War Period

The Greek Revival, 1820–45

Obviously styles in art and fashion do not change overnight, and no period in history has been uniform in appearance. The past lingers and dies slowly; the future is born in the present. Often the old and the new are freely mixed to produce a separate, transitional style worrisome to those who prefer to confine art in neat categories. This has probably never been so clearly demonstrated as in the later decades of the nineteenth century. Before the end of that era the terminology used to categorize the many styles that were competing for public attention had become thoroughly confused.

For more than half a century after the end of the Revolution neoclassical designs in one variation after another had led American fashions in architecture and the decorative arts. No other basic style, before or after, endured for so long. As late as 1850 one observer noted that "the furniture most generally used in private houses is some modification of the classical style," even though totally divergent fashions were already securing a strong position in the marketplace at the time.

Toward the end of the early Federal period the relatively light, delicate forms and geometric shapes inspired by the initial publications of Hepplewhite and Sheraton gave way to bolder contours and more richly carved decoration reflecting French Empire and English Regency taste. The transition may be seen in an elegant New York armchair painted red and gold (Fig. 244). The straight lines and delicate ornament of the early Federal period began to give way to curves and decorative motifs that are broader and bolder. Some of the examples by Phyfe, Lannuier, and others that have already been described exemplify this more assertive neoclassicism as well. There was also an increasing tendency to rely upon ancient Greek, Roman, and Egyptian patterns of form and decoration. These were copied or construed from a variety of English and French publications that were available to the American public and, of course, to the craftsmen who served its wants and needs. Important sources for the new style were Sheraton's later designs; the designs of Thomas Hope and George Smith, which shaped the course of the English Regency; and such periodicals as Rudolph Ackermann's *The Repository of Arts . . .* , and Pierre de la Més-

angère's *Collection de Meubles et Objets de Goût*, published in France.

An outstanding illustration of this trend is a chair, one of a set of eleven made in Baltimore between 1815 and 1820, possibly by John and Hugh Finlay (Fig. 245). The curves of its backrest and back rails are modeled on those of the klismos form of ancient Greece, often depicted in vase paintings of the fifth century B.C. Its painted decoration, gold with green and black, includes ancient Greek motifs, some of which vary from piece to piece in the set. Benjamin Henry Latrobe, architect of the Capitol, designed a similar suite of furniture, probably based on designs in Hope's publications, for a room in Dolly Madison's White House. He commissioned the Finlays to make the suite, for which the drawings still exist. In 1811 Washington Irving described the finished room as one of "blazing splendor"—unfortunately a prophetic phrase, for three years later, during the War of 1812, all those appointments went up in flames when the British put a torch to the building.

What was called a "Grecian" sofa in an early nineteenth-century London price book shows this interpretation of the antique style in its most graceful form (Fig. 246). The continuously and gently flowing curves of the back and arms, the latter lightly carved in a scaly pattern, epitomize the inherent grace of the style. The shape of the dolphin legs and of the carved and gilded leafy sprays that join them to the seat-rail complement the curves of arm and back. An inlaid brass Greek-key pattern whose bright color is echoed in the brass rosettes that terminate the scrolled ends of the back rail provides a strong accent. In its sophisticated conception and the

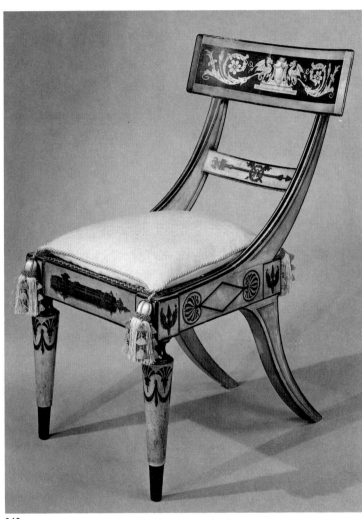

244

245

Fig. 244. Armchair, *New York, about 1820; maple, beech, painted and gilded, height 33½ inches (84.5 cm.). Delicacy of line and proportion triumph in this chair, even though it contains robust elements of the oncoming Greek Revival style. The curved crest rail and the sweeping curves of the arm and arm supports are both features of the later style, but the tapering legs and refined ormolu and painted ornament remain to testify to the linear elegance of early Federal design. The chair belongs to an early nineteenth-century category called "fancy furniture"—highly decorative painted pieces that, at their best, are among the most elegant survivals of the period. They were often made in sets for use in the parlor or dining room. About 1815,*

both Thomas Ash and John Cowperthwaite advertised similar painted furniture in New York newspapers.
Rogers Fund, 1945 (45.151.1)

Fig. 245. Side chair, *attributed to John and Hugh Finlay (w. 1799–1833), Baltimore, 1815–30; maple painted gold with black and green decoration, height 34 inches (86.4 cm.). The broad, sweeping curves of the Greek Revival style are masterfully employed in this modified klismos chair. Its classical prototype, a Roman version of the original Greek klismos chair (today most readily visible in ancient vase paintings), substituted round, tapering front legs for the*

vivid saber curve of the Greek version. One of a set of eleven equally dashing chairs (undoubtedly there were originally twelve), this belongs to a group of distinguished fancy furniture made in early nineteenth-century Baltimore. The design on the broad crest rail of this and the other chairs in this set was very probably taken from Plate 56 of Sheraton's The Cabinet-maker and Upholsterer's Drawing-Book, *1802 edition.*
Purchase, Mrs. Paul Moore Gift, 1965 (65.167.6)

Fig. 246. Sofa, *probably New York, about 1820; mahogany, ash, maple, pine, brass, length 97⅜ inches (247.3 cm.). Flowing curves and a variety of rich and colorful materials are expertly combined in this "dolphin" sofa to create one of the most interesting and graceful pieces of the Greek Revival period. The form itself was shown in an 1802 edition of the* London Chair-Makers' and Carvers' Book of Prices for Workmanship, *but this version, with polished mahogany, inlaid brass Greek key, carved and gilded leaf sprays, and carved verde antique dolphins and scales, is a distinctive high-style New York interpretation.* Friends of the American Wing Fund, 1965 (65.58)

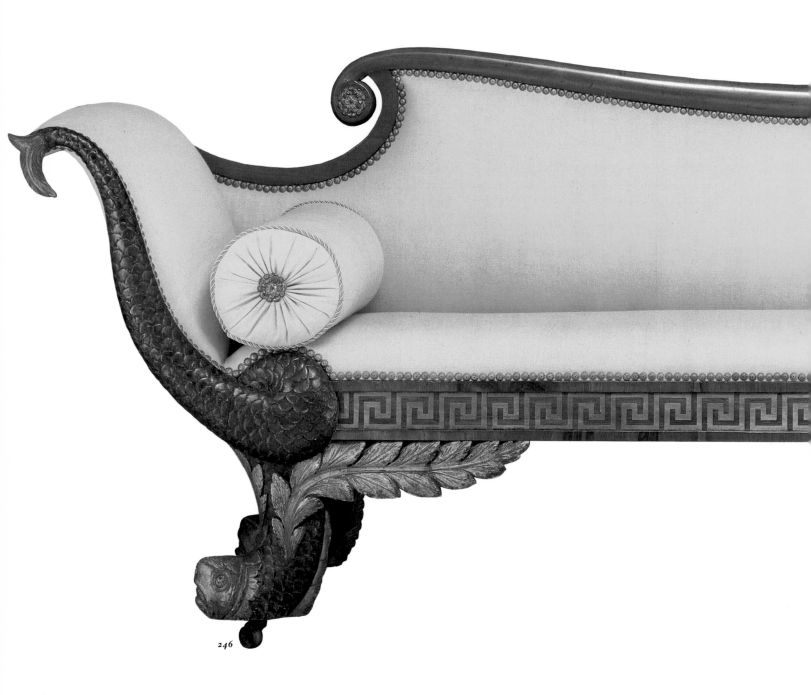

246

superb virtuosity of its workmanship, this piece represents a high point in the development of the Greek Revival, or American Empire, style. With the passing years pieces became heavier in construction and bolder in outline, a drift that can be detected in a mahogany sofa that, in comparison with the dolphin sofa, is a form of impressive bulk (Fig. 247). It was made in Boston about 1825–29. The brass rosette pulls on the arms open cylindrical drawers, each labeled by William Hancock. A half dozen other known pieces carrying Hancock's label are of the style and period of this piece.

Except for some continued references to Greek motifs in decoration, the dependence upon antique forms became less and less visible as the years passed. The piano was, of course, an instrument unknown to the ancients, but an example acquired by the Museum almost a century ago stands on heavy legs and is ornamented by stenciled designs inspired by classical motifs. Made of rosewood about 1825, this handsome instrument displays a gilded tablet with black script letters indicating that it was made by Loud and Brothers, whose firm had been making pianos in Philadelphia since 1816 (Fig. 248).

About the same time the piano was made, a New York cabinetmaking firm, possibly Joseph Meeks and Sons, fashioned a large mahogany secretary that

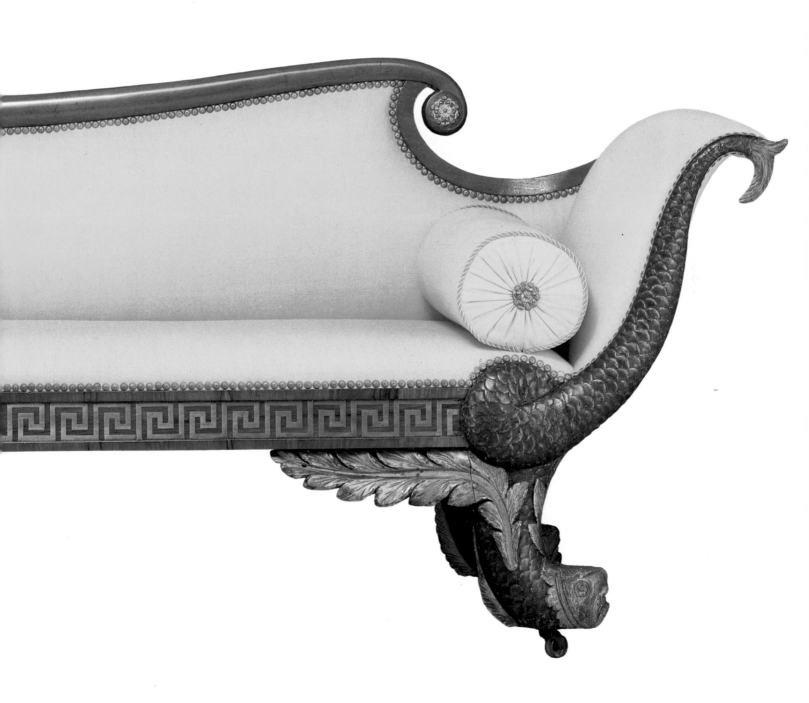

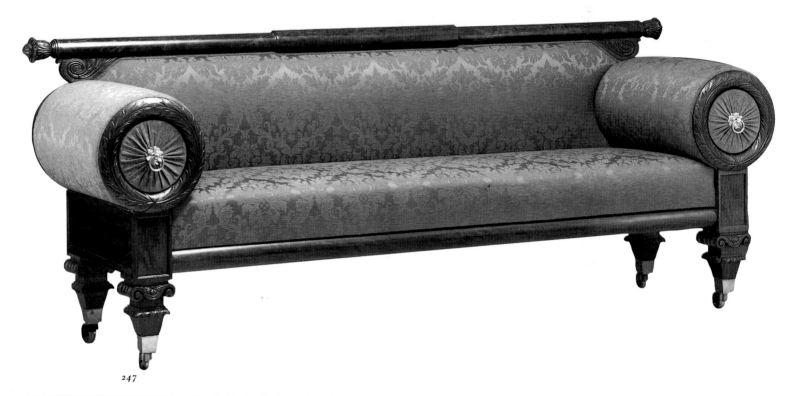

247

248

272

273

Fig. 273. Library table, *attributed to Leon Marcotte (w. New York 1848–about 1880), New York, about 1860; amboyna wood, bird's-eye maple veneer, stained hornbeam, ebonized black cherry, walnut, ash, length 49⅞ inches (126.7 cm.). More restrained than the cabinet in Fig. 272, but bolder than the Louis XVI style on which it was modeled, this elegant table was perhaps part of a set that included chairs, a sofa, and cabinets as well. Leon Marcotte was another of the French émigré cabinetmakers who produced most of the finest furniture in Victorian New York. This table and related pieces are in the Louis XVI Revival style, which had become popular in France before 1840 and was introduced to America by the French and German cabinetmakers who set up business in New York.*
Gift of Mrs. Robert W. de Forest, 1934 (34.140.1)

Fig. 274. Center table, *attributed to Pottier and Stymus (established 1859), New York, 1870–75; rosewood, walnut, length 47 inches (119.4 cm.). Egyptian motifs had become popular during Napoleon's Egyptian campaign of 1798 and had remained in the eclectic nineteenth-century decorative vocabulary thereafter. When exotic styles of all kinds became fashionable after the Civil War, extravagant and colorful Egyptian Revival furniture like this table was made for very high-style interiors. Pottier and Stymus, one of the leading interior decorating firms of the day, specialized in this particular style. Their use of boldly sculptured sphinx heads and vivid inlay, incising, and painting of Egyptian motifs caused one contemporary to adjudge "the style horrible," at the same time that he praised the firm's work as "good."* Purchase, Anonymous Gift, 1968 (68.207)

riod, it is nevertheless an excellent simulation of the French classical mode of the late eighteenth century. The table's most outstanding feature is its top of amboyna veneer bordered with alternating bands of stained hornbeam and amboyna outlined in ivory stringing, with ivory leaves and scrolls inlaid in the corners. This kind of decorative marquetry had been popular in France during the reign of Louis XVI and was revived in France before Marcotte came to the United States in 1840.

The romantic nostalgia that had bred and sustained the Gothic Revival went ever further afield for its satisfactions as the century progressed. No style was too bizarre or too exotic to find its place in the vocabulary of design. Whatever was remote in time or space appealed to the sensibilities of a generation that was be-

ginning to face the unsettling realities of the Industrial Revolution. The mechanization of America had been rapidly accelerated during the years surrounding the Civil War and had brought those realities into sharper focus. "It was no accident," wrote Lewis Mumford, "that caused romanticism and industrialization to appear at the same time. They were rather the two faces of the new civilization, one looking towards the past, and the other towards the future; one glorifying the new, the other clinging to the old; industrialization intent on increasing the physical means of subsistence, romanticism living in a sickly fashion on the hollow glamour of the past."

Among nostalgic and exotic references Egyptian motifs played a persistent role, in architecture as well as in

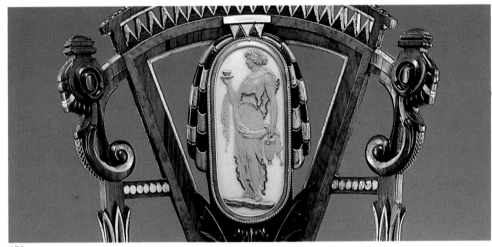

275

furnishings. In 1831 an impressive gate in the Egyptian manner was raised at the entrance to the famous Mount Auburn Cemetery at Cambridge, Massachusetts—to be followed by numerous analogous constructions at other graveyards across the country. Towns along the Mississippi River, "the American Nile" as it was sometimes called, were given names like Cairo, Karnak, Thebes, and Memphis.

In 1852 the first major collection of Egyptian art and artifacts was brought to New York. And about that same time a series of systematic excavations was undertaken in Egypt. Verdi's *Aida*, commissioned to celebrate the opening of the Suez Canal in 1869, was first performed in New York three years later. In 1881, the obelisk commonly known as Cleopatra's Needle was erected in New York's Central Park. The combination of these events encouraged a revival of interest in Egyptian decoration during the 1860s and 1870s. A rosewood table with a variegated marble top, probably made in New York about then, displays carved and gilded sphinx heads at the tops of its four corner supports (Fig. 274). Carved animal paws, a hawklike winged ornament on the apron, and palmette and lotus designs are additional Egyptian Revival details that are superimposed upon this otherwise Renaissance Revival form. It is one of the most impressive examples of this exotic type of furniture in the Museum's collection, which is rich in Egyptian Revival material.

Egyptian motifs also dominate a low side chair (Fig. 277) whose basic form is Renaissance Revival, but whose stylized wings, animal paws, sphinx heads, and geometric motifs were unmistakably inspired by Egyptian design; they are

combined to produce an arresting and exotic object. Equally eye-catching is a side chair also attributed to the high-style firm of Pottier and Stymus (Figs. 275 and 276). It is of laminated and inlaid wood with an enameled porcelain plaque containing a low-relief Greek maiden centered in the back.

The delicate low-relief classical ornament inspired by the Louis XVI period is seen again in an ebonized armchair with ormolu and gilt ornament (Fig. 278) and in a slipper chair that was possibly made by Herter Brothers, like Pottier and Stymus one of Marcotte's competitors and an outstanding New York firm (Fig. 279). While the ultimate inspiration for this chair was eighteenth-century France, its immediate inspiration was the furniture made for Eugénie and Louis Napoleon during France's Second Empire. Light woods and classical designs delicately applied were hallmarks of the style, which was introduced to wealthy Americans by firms such as Herter Brothers that had close connections with European furniture makers. A chair that makes more lavish use of inlay is the ebonized-maple side chair with delicate mother-of-pearl designs (Fig. 280).

By the 1870s the day of the professional interior decorator, designer, and supplier had dawned. "We generally get a house from the mason, that is when the mason work has been finished, and have charge of the entire woodwork decoration," wrote a representative of one firm that specialized in such commissions. ". . . Sometimes we get *carte blanche* for everything—style, design, quality and price." He spoke for Pottier and Stymus, examples of whose output may be seen again in two walnut chairs made for exhibition at the Centennial

celebration (Fig. 282). Pottier described the chairs as "in the style of Henry II," who reigned over France in the sixteenth century; their only readily apparent connection to Henry, however, is the use of his cipher and that of his mistress, Diane de Poitiers, in the designs of the tapestry upholstery. For the rest, they provide another example of the nineteenth-century inventions that were arbitrarily labeled Renaissance.

The eclectic character of the period can be seen in a number of other forms. The design of a particularly handsome stool (Fig. 281) made and labeled by the versatile Alexander Roux about 1865 is of a style termed by one contemporary "neo grec." It recalls the ancient curule seating forms that had influenced Duncan Phyfe earlier in the century. Here, however, hocked animal legs with waterleaf carvings terminate in gilded hooves. On either side of the piece is a pointed arch filled with turned-spindle ribs, shapes that resemble highly stylized palmettes. Polychrome decoration and the original tufted brocade upholstery give added distinction to this unusual and exotic example of stylish furniture.

Figs. 275–82. Chairs. *Along with a continuing fascination with revival styles, Americans of the last third of the nineteenth century felt an increasing interest in the exotic. This gallery of chairs, of the Renaissance, Louis XVI, and Egyptian Revival styles, as well as the Neo-Grec, were all very fashionable and were made more or less concurrently. Materials and decorative techniques vary widely and this, too, is characteristic of the age.*

Figs. 275 and 276. *Side chair, attributed to Pottier and Stymus (established 1859), New York, about 1875; detail (Fig. 275) on p. 179; laminated woods, including walnut and mahogany, enameled porcelain medallion, height 37⅛ inches (94.3 cm.).*
Purchase, Charlotte Pickman-Gertz Gift, 1983 (1983.68)

Fig. 277. *Side chair, attributed to Pottier and Stymus (established 1859), New York, 1870–75; rosewood, prickly juniper veneer, ash, height 28⅛ inches (71.4 cm.).*
Funds from various donors, 1970 (1970.35.2)

Fig. 278. *Armchair, attributed to Leon Marcotte (w. New York 1848–about 1880), New York, about 1860; ebonized maple and fruitwood, ormolu, height 39 inches (99.1 cm.).*
Gift of Mrs. D. Chester Noyes, 1968 (68.69.2)

Fig. 279. *Slipper chair, attributed to Herter Brothers (mid-1860s–1882), New York, about 1865; maple, rosewood, height 30¼ inches (76.8 cm.).*
Gift of James Graham and Sons, 1965 (65.186)

Fig. 280. *Side chair, attributed to Leon Marcotte (w. New York 1848–about 1880), New York, 1865–70; ebonized maple, brass, mother-of-pearl, height 35¾ inches (90.8 cm.).*
Gift of Ronald S. Kane, 1968 (68.198.2)

Fig. 281. *Stool, by Alexander Roux (w. New York 1837–81), New York, about 1865; painted beech, height 23¾ inches (60.3 cm.).*
Purchase, The Edgar J. Kaufmann Foundation Gift, 1969 (69.108)

Fig. 282. *Armchair, by Pottier and Stymus (established 1859), New York, about 1875; black walnut, height 51¾ inches (131.5 cm.).*
Gift of Auguste Pottier, 1888 (88.10.3)

277

276

278

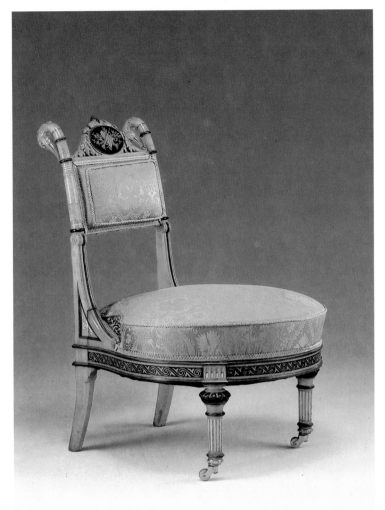

279

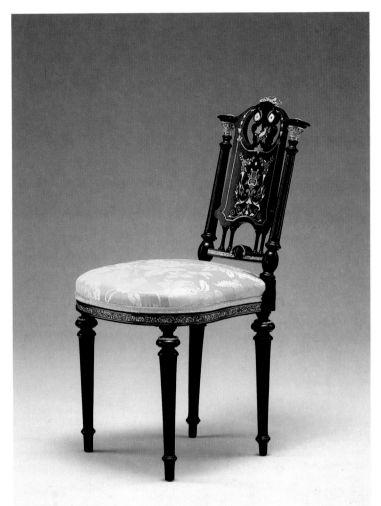

280

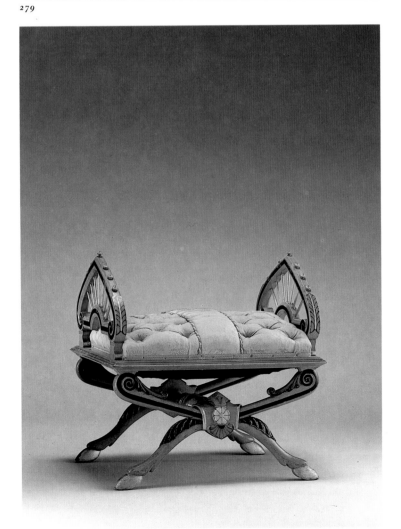

281

282

Innovative Furniture

283

Throughout the nineteenth century a variety of furniture was made in America that had little or no reference to the prevailing formal styles of the period. As early as the first decade of the century one Samuel Gragg of Boston patented a uniquely conceived chair (Fig. 283) whose seat and legs were single pieces of wood bent into graceful shapes, forecasting the bentwood furniture that became vastly popular later in the century.

What may well be a unique piece, probably intended for use as a barber's chair, combines a variety of disparate elements (Figs. 284–86). Most prominently, the right arm broadens out into a writing surface similar to those occasionally found on Windsors. In this case the surface displays an inlaid design of a mariner's compass, indicating that it may have served on shipboard. As an added convenience a drawer is fitted beneath the seat, also a feature of some Windsors. The painted crest rail resembles those that were commonly used on the so-called Boston rockers that evolved in New England in the 1820s and remained popular for years to come. The chair's raking front legs are connected by a carved and gilded stretcher.

It was an inventive age, and some furniture makers, with typical American aptitude for mechanical improvisation, took advantage of newly developed techniques and newly available materials to create unprecedented forms that added diversity and fresh interest to the decorative arts of their time.

Cast iron was an inexpensive and durable material for all kinds of utilitarian objects. Always less expensive than wrought iron because it was made in molds rather than hammered by hand, cast iron had been used in the eighteenth century for such small necessary objects as pots, andirons, firebacks, and stove plates, and it was a natural material from which to manufacture stoves as increasingly efficient models were developed during the late eighteenth and early nineteenth centuries. As the nineteenth century progressed the material began to be used for a wider variety of forms. A small, useful cast-iron object that combines classical and rococo motifs is the music rack of 1835–50—the only known example of this form (Fig. 287).

Advances in iron founding and milling techniques in the middle decades of the nineteenth century made it possible to fashion an increasing variety of forms in designs that followed any and all of the prevailing styles. Chairs, settees, urns, and many other elaborately patterned forms were made in cast iron for use in the garden. The Museum's collection of such pieces contains representative designs in the eclectic styles that succeeded one another and intermixed from the 1840s to the end of the century.

The use of metal in the fabrication of chairs led designers in diverse experimental directions. The point is illustrated by an unusual patented side chair intricately put together of cast- and wrought-iron and wood with an upholstered seat (Fig. 288). This ingenious construction, a so-called centripetal chair, was produced by the American Chair Company of Troy, New York, manufacturer of reclining seats for railroad passenger cars. The crown-shaped wrought-iron base acts as a spring that permits the occupant to recline or sit up as he chooses. The iron frame of the back is "japanned" (covered with a

284

285

Figs. 284–86. Writing/barber chair, *Boston, 1820–25; mahogany, inlay, and painted decoration, height 42 inches (106.7 cm.). Multipurpose furniture has always intrigued buyers, and this chair is an odd mixture of writing-arm Windsor and barber chair. The curved, painted crest rail is removable, and there is an insert with a curving headpiece that could be used when the sitter needed a shave. The mixture of decorative techniques is odd, too: fancy-chair painted ornament is joined, on the writing arm, with mahogany and light-wood inlay in the shape of a compass. The back and seat are upholstered in a cut-velvet fabric that is a close facsimile of the original, over the original coil springs, a highly unusual feature on a chair of this early date.* Sansbury-Mills Fund, 1976 (1976.50)

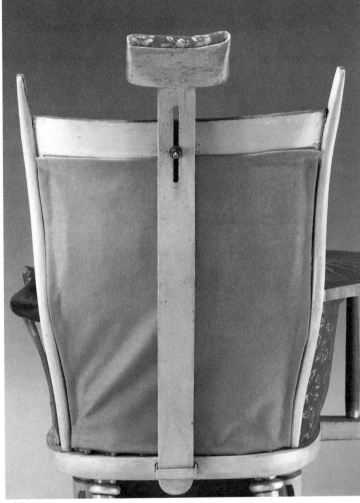

286

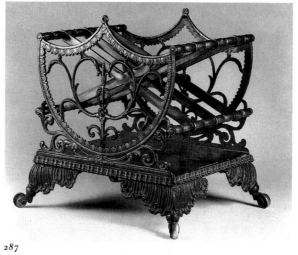

287

288

hard, brilliant varnish) with polychrome decoration surrounded by gilt scrolls. Several variations of this remarkable contrivance were represented at the London Crystal Palace exhibition of 1851.

Folding furniture of one kind or another was in use from ancient times. Earlier in this book it was noted that from the first days of settlement American colonists had resorted to such space-saving features, as indeed we continue to do today. In the meantime, the nineteenth century provided fresh opportunities for mechanical inventions along these lines. In 1876 the Marks Adjustable Folding Chair Company of New York patented a reclining armchair with a strap-metal frame and folding foot piece (Fig. 289). This seat, which might aptly be called a chaise longue, has an arched, paneled, and incised top rail crowning the adjustable back—a decorative touch reflecting the Renaissance Revival style of the period.

New wire-making machines provided elements for the twisted-wire garden furniture that was another popular novelty in the years following the Civil War

289

Fig. 289. Armchair, *by the Marks Adjustable Folding Chair Company (1877–97), about 1876; walnut, metal, cane, height 45¾ inches (116.2 cm.). Folding stools and chairs were known to the Egyptians, the Greeks, and the Romans. Later civilizations occasionally employed the form but, in the last quarter of the nineteenth century, the adjustable folding chair reappeared in a dramatically increased number of versions. This one, with adjustable arms and a folding foot-rest, is constructed of lightweight materials and mounted on casters so that it can be moved easily from place to place. Its maker listed a number of uses for the chair, including that of supporting an invalid—for which it seems especially well suited.*
Sage Fund, 1975 (1975.157)

Fig. 290. Settee, *United States, about 1870; wire and solid metal rod, height 38 inches (96.5 cm.). This twisted-wire garden seat, which retains its original blue-green finish, belongs to an innovative group made possible by the invention of wire-making machines. The malleability of wire invited designers to indulge in extravagantly curvaceous designs. Like cast-iron furniture, these whimsical wire seats were eminently practical for the garden, but they were also fairly fragile and relatively few have survived.*
Sansbury-Mills Fund, 1982 (1982.122)

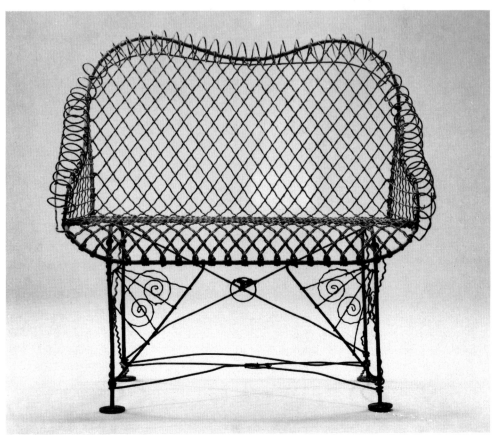

290

Fig. 291. *Armchair*, by George Hunzinger (1835–98), New York, about 1876; maple, fabric-covered steel mesh, height 34 inches (86.4 cm.). About mid-century, Hunzinger came to New York from Germany, where his family had been furniture makers for centuries. He was fascinated with furniture that actually had moving parts, or seemed to, and he patented many innovations, including that of using woven-steel bands instead of conventional upholstery. The bands of this chair are covered with blue fabric and the wooden frame is composed of elements that look like parts of machines—a Hunzinger trademark. Another innovation is that of cantilevering the seat from the back legs—a technique that became important in twentieth-century chair construction.
Sansbury-Mills Fund, 1982 (1982.69)

292

Fig. 292. *Side chair,* Toledo Metal Furniture Company, 1900–15; chrome on steel, Leatherette, height 34½ inches (87.6 cm.). This handsome metal version of the graceful, lightweight bentwood chair introduced by Michael Thonet retains its paper label and original Leatherette seat. The steel strips of which it was made were produced by machine, and the chair was thus inexpensive enough for ice-cream parlors across the land to use—thus its nickname "ice-cream parlor chair."
Gift of Jonathan Holstein and Gail van der Hoof, 1979 (1979.189)

(Fig. 290). The fanciful designs of these pieces recall those of Rococo Revival objects; the use of wire foreshadows that of designers like Harry Bertoia, whose welded-wire "diamond chairs" became popular after World War II.

Another innovative metal form was the "ice-cream" chair, so called because its portability and inexpensiveness made it practical for use in luncheonettes and ice-cream parlors everywhere. Some were made of wire and others, like this one, were made of wider metal strips curved like Thonet's bentwood (Fig. 292).

In the 1860s George Hunzinger of New York, one of the many German furniture makers who emigrated to America in the middle years of the century, patented an assortment of chairs, some of which could be folded up (Fig. 291) and some that only appeared to be collapsible. All were inventive in their unusual and complicated designs, which suggested the cogs, wheels, and shafts of a machine that might be set in motion at a moment's notice. The example here illustrated is made of walnut and carries the label "Hunzinger/N.Y./ Pat. March 30/1869." It bears an unmistakable imprint of the machine age, and at the same time of a highly individualistic designer.

Intricately structured furnishings made of rattan and wicker had been imported from the Orient from the first days of America's trade with China. Even earlier, examples had found their way to this country: it is said that a wicker cradle was among the limited cargo of household gear in the *Mayflower*; and an inventory from the Adam Thoroughgood house, the oldest surviving house in Virginia, lists "one wicker chair for a child." "Wicker" is a

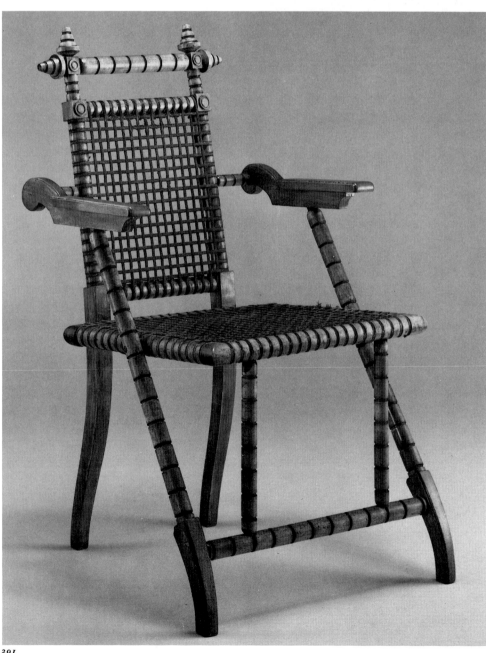

291

subtle outlines were influenced by the Anglo-Japanese designs of E. W. Godwin, a leading English figure in the Aesthetic movement and an enthusiastic admirer of Japanese arts and architecture. Oscar Wilde, who along with Whistler was one of Godwin's patrons, called him "the greatest aesthete of them all."

Bamboo furniture from the Orient was an absorbing fashion of the time, and rising demand for this exotic product very soon resulted in the domestic manufacture of simulated-bamboo pieces. Generally made of maple turned and ringed on a lathe to resemble the natural fibrous material, "bamboo" elements were combined to produce conventional stylish Western forms of the period. The point is emphatically made by a bedroom suite probably made in the 1880s and consisting of a bed, a chest of drawers, a dressing table, chairs, and other pieces unknown in oriental art but suitable for Western comfort and convenience (Fig. 300). Each element of the suite follows the rectilinear lines of the current mode, with panels of figured bird's-eye maple and galleries of spindles in the Eastlake manner. Such mixtures of material and motifs, according to one contemporary observer, resulted in an interior that was "light and bright, summery and inviting."

Another example of the variety of exotic influences that affected late nineteenth-century styles is a clock, almost nine feet high, that was fashioned by Tiffany and Company in 1882 (Fig. 301). This extraordinary timepiece in the Near Eastern style is almost the last word in eclecticism. The case is topped by a brass dome ornamented with stars and crescents following Turkish, Persian, and Indian models; and an almost indescribable variety of other design elements ornaments the case. Quite aside from these fanciful features brilliantly executed in wood and metal, the clock is a horological phenomenon in its mechanical ingenuity. A pendulum containing mercury regulates the movement regardless of the fluctuations of temperature and barometric pressure.

Louis Comfort Tiffany, son of the founder of Tiffany and Company, began his varied career as an artist. As he was turning twenty-one he went to Paris to study painting, and then on to North

302

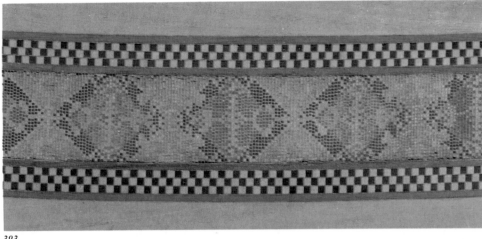

303

Figs. 302 and 303. Armchair, attributed to Louis Comfort Tiffany (1848–1933), New York, 1890–1900; ash, wood and brass inlay, height 35⅝ inches (90.5 cm.). Tiffany endowed this French bergère (closed-arm chair) with Art Nouveau and exotic Eastern motifs, so that it became a form totally of its time. Low-relief carved flowers on the crest rail suggest asymmetrical Art Nouveau designs, while the inlaid geometrical motifs that descend the arms and form a band across the front and side seat-rails employ the east Indian technique of inlaying minuscule pieces of wood in fine patterns. The legs, tapered and reeded in the eighteenth-century tradition, end in feet made of glass balls held in place by brass claws—a type of foot found on other pieces associated with Tiffany.
Gift of Mr. and Mrs. Georges E. Seligmann, 1964 (64.202.1)

Fig. 304. Cabinet, by George C. Flint and Company, New York, about 1910; mahogany, glass, velvet, height 58¾ inches (149.2 cm.). This curio cabinet in the Art Nouveau style was copied almost exactly from a piece by the well-known French designer Louis Majorelle of Nancy. The Art Nouveau style, which had become popular in Europe before the turn of the century, was never so successful in America, and examples made here tend to be stiffer and to lack the sensuous grace of European designs. This cabinet is closer to European models than most, for American pieces were frequently at least partly machine made and were therefore not so elegantly hand finished as European ones, but even this example lacks the suave flow of the best European pieces. Purchase, Anonymous Gift, 1968 (68.132)

304

Africa and the Near East to widen his vision. In 1875, after returning from a second visit to Paris, he decided to make "decorative work" his main profession. In 1879 he organized the firm Associated Artists, with Samuel Colman, Lockwood de Forest, and Candace Wheeler as the associates. De Forest was an artist and orientalist who founded shops for the revival of woodworking in India to supply his New York studio-salesroom with "artistic creations."

Tiffany's romance with Eastern art, which he so imaginatively and variously expressed in contemporary idioms, was not an exclusive preoccupation in spite of the obvious influence it had on his work. The variety of forms in different mediums that issued from his company and studios is almost incalculable, and is barely suggested by the group of disparate objects shown in this book (see also Figs. 2, 3, and 5). Two ash chairs with reeded legs (Figs. 302 and 303), which may well be from Tiffany's studios, are in the shape of late eighteenth-century French bergères, although their light-wood frames, inlaid motifs, and shallow flower-and-leaf carving are very much in the spirit of the late nineteenth century.

An Art Nouveau cabinet whose flowing lines are related to those of Tiffany's bergères was made by George Flint and Company (Fig. 304). Very similar to a cabinet by the French designer Louis Majorelle, it belongs to what so far seems to be a small group of American furniture in this curvilinear style.

Both L. C. Tiffany and his remarkable younger contemporary, Frank Lloyd Wright, won international renown for their quite different contributions to the artistic movements of their time, contradicting Henry James's snobbish pronouncement that true art must wither in the "cruel air" of America. Among other Americans who also gave a flat lie to that observation was Louis Henri Sullivan, an almost exact contemporary of Tiffany's. In his adopted city of Chicago Sullivan represented a new and vital trend in American architecture, and his structures contributed to the unique distinction the Chicago skyscape was soon enjoying. By reconciling technology and utility with poetry and beauty, Sullivan transformed the steel-framed

Fig. 311. Table, *by Joseph Urban (1872–1933)
for the Wiener Werkstätte of America, New York,
1921; black lacquer, silver leaf, silk panel inset
on top, height 23⅞ inches (60.6 cm.). The ex-
quisite workmanship for which the Wiener Werkstätte stood is present here, in this elegant table
made for the Wiener Werkstätte Showroom on
Fifth Avenue in New York. Severe geometric
shapes are employed in the design, but the ornament is less rigid: a bead-and-reel motif edges the
base of the supporting column and fills in the
narrow slits on the lower half of the column so
that it serves as a kind of stop fluting. Delicately
drawn flowers, leaves, stems, and insects are
gracefully disposed on the tabletop.*
Purchase, Gifts in memory of Emil Blasberg, 1978
(1978.492.1)

Fig. 312. Side chair, *by Frank Lloyd Wright
(1867–1959), 1916–22; oak, cane, height
37¾ inches (95.9 cm.). The only example with
cane panels in an American collection, this chair
was designed by Wright to furnish a promenade
in his Imperial Hotel in Tokyo. Its angled forms
repeated the lines and angles of the space it occupied. The Imperial Hotel was one of Wright's
great engineering triumphs; it was designed so
that it could—and did—withstand severe earth-
quakes. It was, unfortunately, torn down in
1968 and only a fragment of the building and
some of its furnishings survive.*
Gift of Dr. Roger G. Gerry, 1968 (68.20.1)

311

312

SILVER

Fig. 313. Detail, bowl by Cornelius Kierstede,
see Fig. 316.

The Colonial Period 1630–1790

Fig. 315. Chocolate pot, by Edward Winslow (1669–1753), Boston, about 1700–10; silver, height 9⅛ inches (23.2 cm.). New both in its tall lantern shape and in its function of serving chocolate, a recently introduced drink in the colonies, this pot is also decorated in the newly fashionable baroque style. Like the standing salt, it has surfaces that are alternately boldly ornamented and plain, creating highlights and shadows and contrasting smooth and ribbed areas. Cut-card work, in which a flat design is cut out of a separate sheet of silver and applied, is another typical baroque embellishment, used here at the base of the spout and the finial of the domed lid.
Bequest of Alphonso T. Clearwater, 1933 (33.120.221)

314

Fig. 314. Standing salt, by John Allen (1671/ 72–1760) and John Edwards (1671–1746), Boston, about 1700; silver, height 5⅞ inches (14.9 cm.). The spool shape of this standing salt is common to all three surviving American examples of the form and to the earlier seventeenth-century English salts that inspired them. Grand containers of this kind went out of style in America about 1700 as salt became more plentiful and fashionable hostesses began to serve it in individual dishes. The phrase "below the salt," which still denotes lack of status, arose in medieval times when salt was a luxury affordable only by the very rich. It meant that the guest was not seated near the host and the salt, but farther away.
Gift of Sarah Hayward Draper, 1972 (1972.204)

Long before the colonies produced a portrait painter or a landscapist of any consequence, they supported scores of master craftsmen in the precious metals whose work was handsomely designed and scrupulously wrought. The silversmith—or "goldsmith," as he was often termed—was a banker of sorts through whose skills the miscellaneous foreign coins that flowed into America in the course of trade might be converted into useful objects of silver, or, occasionally, gold. The weight and purity of this plate was certified by the integrity of the smith who made and marked it. Such marks and engraved decorations, which often included the initials of the owner, enabled him to clearly identify his tankard, porringer, or spoon in case of loss or theft, as he could never hope to identify coins. The objects could also be put to practical use at table or displayed as conspicuous wealth on a cupboard, and they could easily be reconverted into bullion or coin if need be.

Boston and New York (New Amsterdam until 1664) were the first New World centers of this highly practical art. As might be expected, work turned out in these two separate areas showed marked regional differences in design. Among the earliest colonial items in the collection are several silver shillings and sixpences coined at Boston by English-born John Hull and Robert Sanderson by order of the General Court of Massachusetts, but in defiance of restrictions imposed by Britain. These pioneering smiths worked both in partnership and individually, turning out forms that, except for the marks stamped on them, were indistinguishable from the relatively plain objects produced in England at the time.

By the end of the seventeenth century baroque features associated with the William and Mary style were being expressed in silver—a development clearly observable in a spool-shaped standing salt made in Boston around the turn of the century by John Edwards and John Allen (Fig. 314). Descended from the great architectural salts that were a conspicuous feature of medieval and Renaissance dining boards, this example is ornamented with two bands of spiral gadrooning—that is, convex, or inverted, fluting. Similar bands distinguish a rare chocolate pot made in Boston by Edward Winslow about that same time (Fig. 315). The salt represents a form that was being held over from earlier days and would soon be abandoned, while the chocolate pot is an early example of a form that evolved in England only late in the seventeenth century, when drinking chocolate first became fashionable. Both pieces, however, strongly remind us of the degree of affluence and the taste for luxury that had developed in New England less than a century after the settlement of that Puritan land.

The silver fashioned in New York in the late seventeenth and early eighteenth centuries reflects the mingling of Dutch, English, and French traditions. Cornelius Kierstede, probably the most individualistic of early American craftsmen, was the maker of a boldly embossed six-panel bowl whose design is peculiar to New York (Fig. 316) and a unique pair of stop-fluted candlesticks (Fig. 318). The sticks and a matching snuffer stand have splayed bases chased with fantastic chinoiserie designs. A beaker made by Jurian Blanck, Jr., in about 1683 (Fig. 317) and engraved with a Dutch inscription and figures of

316

Fig. 316. Bowl, *by Cornelius Kierstede (1675–1757), New York, 1700–10; silver, diameter 10 inches (25.4 cm.). This bowl, with six clearly defined lobes filled with repoussé (relief) flowers and leaves and equipped with caryatid handles, belongs to a group of at least eighteen lobed bowls of New York manufacture. The Dutch and Huguenot silversmiths who made them were remembering similar pieces characteristic of northern European silverwork, especially as it was interpreted in Holland, and these in turn had been inspired by Italian mannerist silversmiths of the Renaissance. Their original use, according to John N. Pearce, who studied the group and published his findings in* The Magazine Antiques *(October 1961), was as a container of brandy and raisins. The bowl was passed from one guest to another, and each dipped himself a helping of the compote with the silver spoon supplied by the host. This particular bowl, the most lavishly decorated and one of the largest of its type, bears initials said to be those of New York baker Theunis Jacobsen Quick and his wife, Vroutje, married in 1689.*
Samuel D. Lee Fund, 1938 (38.63)

Fig. 317. Beaker, *attributed to Jurian Blanck, Jr. (about 1645–1714), New York, about 1683; silver, height 7¼ inches (18.4 cm.). Beakers, a common form of drinking vessel in the seventeenth century, were used for both domestic and ecclesiastical purposes. This example is inscribed, in Dutch, "A token of devotion and loyalty to the church in Kingston, 1683." Its graceful tapering shape and its engraved decoration combining rigid strapwork and whimsical floral scrolls are typical of New York beakers which, in turn, reflect seventeenth-century Dutch traditions. The beaker's engraved ovals, containing representations of Faith, Hope, and Charity, are characteristic of New York church-silver ornament.*
Jointly owned by the Reformed Protestant Dutch Church of Kingston, New York, and The Metropolitan Museum of Art, 1933 (33.120.621)

317

Fig. 318. Candlestick and snuffer stand, *by Cornelius Kierstede (1675–1757), New York, 1700–10; silver, height of candlestick 11½ inches (29.2 cm.), height of snuffer 8¼ inches (21 cm.). Kierstede, one of the finest silversmiths of his time, made this snuffer stand and candlestick (which is one of a pair—the other is also in the Museum's collection) for Johannes and Elizabeth Schuyler of Albany, New York. Schuyler was prominent in civic affairs, serving as mayor of Albany from 1703 to 1706. The impressive height of the candlesticks is matched by the boldness of their ornament. Stop-fluted columns, gadrooning, and chinoiserie vignettes combine in a way that both unifies the whole object and provides the contrasts that are so important in baroque design. The snuffer stand, which originally* held a scissors-shaped snuffer for cutting and trimming the wick, has an acorn-shaped support reminiscent of the huge turnings on European state beds and cupboards of the sixteenth and seventeenth centuries. The snuffer stood vertically in the rectangular holder.

Candlestick: Gift of Robert L. Cammann, 1957 (57.153a,b); *snuffer stand:* Gift of Mr. and Mrs. William A. Moore, 1923 (23.80.21)

318

Figs. 319 and 320. Group of tankards: left,
*by Simeon Soumain (1685–1750), New York,
1705–25; silver, height 7⅛ inches (18.1 cm.);*
center, *by Jeremiah Dummer (1645–1718),
Boston, 1690–1705; silver, height 7 inches (17.8
cm.);* right, *by Benjamin Burt (1729–1805),
Boston, 1760–70; silver, height 8½ inches
(21.6 cm.). Throughout the colonial period and
well into the Federal, widely separated American
cities produced similar forms but decorated them
differently. That point is brought out here, where
two tankards of the early colonial period share a
low, broad body, wide curved handle, and flat
stepped top. The New England example on the
left, however, lacks the rich ornament of the New
York version, having only cut-card ornament at*

the base of the handle and on the lid as opposed to the band of leaf molding and meander wire at the base and rich cast ornament on the handle of the New York piece. Both have cast masks applied to their handle terminals and scrolled thumbpieces on their lids, but the tight single scroll of New York is quite different from the more relaxed double scrolls of New England. Such differences were very likely the result of craft specialization, in which one craftsman made thumbpieces and sold them to his fellow workers. The later example, on the right, made in Boston in the late colonial period, shows the preferred tankard form in that city after mid-century. The body is now elongated, the thrust is vertical, and the lid has become a high dome and acquired a

decorative finial. Rococo engraving provides the only other embellishment, except for the single horizontal band that encircles the tankard slightly below midpoint. By comparison, New York tankards of this period remain low and broad and look much as they had earlier. Their trend was toward simplicity, away from the earlier decorative leaf bands and cast ornament.

Gift of Annie Clarkson, 1927 (27.85.1); Anonymous Gift, 1934 (34.16); Gift of Robert S. Grinnel, 1970 (1970.287.1)

Faith, Hope, and Charity represents a type of vessel used for both domestic and sacramental purposes. A small, handsomely decorated globular teapot by Jacob Boelen is the earliest known American example of this form (Fig. 321). It was made at a time when tea, like coffee, was still a rare, exotic, and expensive commodity.

From the beginning American colonists preferred beer and ale to water, though they were not always able to indulge their preference. Describing his own situation in 1629, the Reverend Francis Higginson of Salem wrote: "Whereas my stomach could only digest and did require such drink as was both strong and stale, I can and ofttimes do drink New England water very well." Silver tankards, capacious and broad based to hold generous draughts of spirituous beverages, were at first straight sided and flat topped. The earliest New England examples often have cut-card ornament (flat designs cut into decorative shapes and applied), gadrooning, plain ribbed moldings, and cast thumbpieces (Fig. 319, right). Early tankards made in New York were also capacious, flat topped, and broad based (Fig. 319, left). With their engraved lids, corkscrew-shaped thumbpieces, handles with applied cast masks and garlands, and ornamental base moldings, these handsome drinking vessels display a combination of decorative features peculiar to New York. Flat tops for their tankards continued to please New Yorkers, but New Englanders came to prefer drinking from examples with domed tops (Fig. 320).

The suave simplicity of the Queen Anne style is handsomely demonstrated in two silver teapots—one with a pear-shaped body, the other globular (Figs.

320

321

322

Fig. 342. Vase, *designed by John T. Curran for Tiffany and Company (1853–present), New York, 1893; silver, gold, and enamel, height 31 inches (78.7 cm). The opulence characteristic of the highest style objects of the late nineteenth century is exemplified in this piece, made for the World's Columbian Exposition of 1893 and called the "Magnolia vase." Its size is impressive, its materials precious, its ornament lavish and varied. Wildly eclectic design influences are incorporated in it: a contemporary described the piece, saying that its form had been suggested by "pieces of pottery found among the relics of the* ancient cliff-dwellers of the Pueblos," and calling its handles Toltec. Its base employs curves in the Art Nouveau manner, and its ornament is symbolic of American plants and other natural forms. Yet, despite its disparate influences, it is cohesive—it succeeds as a work of art.
Gift of Mrs. Winthrop Atwell, 1899 (99.2)

Fig. 343. Presentation vase, *designed by Paulding Farnham for Tiffany and Company (1853–present), New York, 1893–95; gold, semiprecious stones, and enamel, height 19½ inches (49.5 cm). The height of lavishness, this vase could have been produced only in a period of prosperity, optimism, and self-confidence. It was commissioned by the stockholders and direc-* tors of the American Cotton Oil Company as a gift to Edward Dean Adams, chairman of the board. Adams had labored ceaselessly to save the company from ruin, refusing all compensation, and this was a thank-you gesture. Its form is that of an ancient Greek vase, and its symbolism is that of traditional mythology, employed here to tell the story of cotton and the American Cotton Oil Company. It was so necessary to have a key to the symbolism that Tiffany published a booklet to explain it and, while they were at it, added remarkable statistics on the large number of specialized craftsmen needed to make this tour de force and emphasized its great cost.
Gift of Edward D. Adams, 1904 (04.1)

344

In 1874, to honor William Cullen Bryant on the occasion of his eightieth birthday, a group of the poet's friends commissioned James H. Whitehouse of Tiffany and Company to fashion a huge vase in the Renaissance Revival style (Fig. 341). Although this massive piece has the outlines of an antique Greek vase, it is overlaid with complex ornamentation that includes a profile portrait of Bryant, symbolic representations of American flora and fauna, and Renaissance Revival medallions referring to the poet's writings and interests.

Bryant gave the vase to the Museum a few years after it was presented to him.

Tiffany's designers worked in a wide range of styles, often combining influences from several sources in one piece. A creamer and sugar bowl (Fig. 344), for example, add Japanese and "Eastlake" motifs to a basically Renaissance Revival shape.

Fig. 344. Cream pitcher and sugar bowl, *by Tiffany and Company (1853–present), New York, 1874; silver, height of sugar bowl 4¹⁵⁄₁₆ inches (12.3 cm.), height of creamer 4⅝ inches (11.2 cm.). The helmet-shaped creamer and the high loop handles of both pieces are characteristic of Renaissance Revival design, but the flat applied fish, lily pads, and shells, as well as the engraved seaweed and lily-pad stems evoke Japanese art—a great influence on Western designers in the 1870s. A further diverse influence is seen in the flat handle supports with cutout designs, for they resemble "Eastlake" furniture motifs.*
Purchase, The Edgar J. Kaufmann Foundation Gift, 1969 (69.128.1,2)

The Post-Centennial Period 1875–1915

By the time the foregoing pieces were made, Tiffany's silverwares were already internationally acclaimed. At the Paris exposition of 1867 the firm had won the first award ever given to a foreigner. In their opulence, eclecticism, and use of symbolism, two other large and impressive vases made by Tiffany and Company represent the extravagant taste of America's Gilded Age. The complexity of design of both the so-called Magnolia vase and the Adams vase (Figs. 342 and 343) is staggering, calling for expert craftsmanship of a kind that could probably not be commanded today. About this same time Tiffany and Company produced a teapot (Fig. 345; part of a so-called tête-à-tête set) that was much less grand than the vases in conception, but of a highly imaginative design. The company described the set as ". . . made . . . entirely by hand . . . without seams . . . each . . . from a single piece of silver. It is enameled, etched and gilded; and is also etched and gilded on the interior, which in itself is a very difficult and remarkable piece of work. . . ." This exotic set was clearly inspired by Islamic art: the colors of the enamels recall those of Turkish rugs and of Syrian Mamluk glass of the fourteenth century. The influence of the East is seen again in a tray ornamented with iris blooms and leaves—a theme taken from Japanese art and used here in combination with a hand-hammered surface that is one of the characteristics of the Arts and Crafts movement (Fig. 346).

A ewer and plateau (Fig. 347) made early in the present century by the Gorham Manufacturing Company of Providence, Rhode Island, were fashioned in the Art Nouveau style. Martelé was Gorham's name for handmade wares of

345

346

Fig. 352. Basin, by Joseph Leddell, Sr. (about 1690–1754) or Joseph Leddell, Jr. (d. 1754), New York, 1712–54; pewter, diameter 12⅞ inches (32.7 cm.). Basins were used in colonial times both for serving food and for baptismal rites. It is not known for which purpose this basin was originally made, but whatever its use, it is a splendid example of its type, rare because it is the earliest form of American basin and because of the perfection of its shape. Joseph Sr. is thought to have been born in England, where he no doubt learned his trade. He was in New York by 1711, conducting business there until his death in 1754. His son, Joseph Jr., who undoubtedly learned the craft from his father, was at work in New York from about 1740 until his death in 1754. He advertised in 1752 that he made "any uncommon Thing in Pewter, in any Shape or Form as shall be order'd. . . ." It is unclear whether the basin was made by father or son, for it is marked simply "I. Leddell."
Gift of Mrs. J. Insley Blair, 1940 (40.184.2)

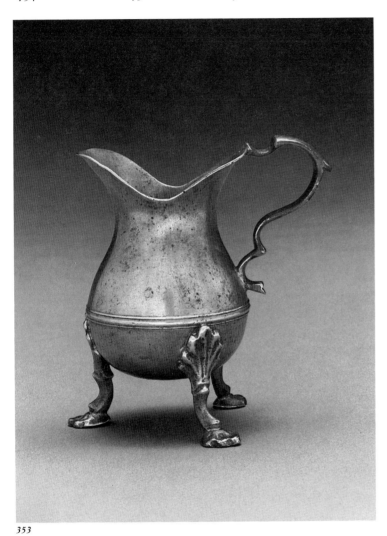

353

354

Fig. 353. Creamer, by Peter Young (1749–1813), New York and Albany, 1775–95; pewter, height 4½ inches (10.5 cm.). Pear-shaped pitchers like this with scroll handle, cabriole legs, and shell feet are rare in American pewter. They incorporate fashionable rococo features that were seldom seen in pewter, for they necessitated buying costly new molds. Peter Young, wrote Ledlie Laughlin in Pewter in America, "was not just another pewterer. He was a maker of taste, ability, and considerable originality."
Gift of Clara Lloyd-Smith Weber, 1981 (1981.117)

Fig. 354. Measure, by Boardman and Hart (1828–53), New York, 1835; pewter, height 7 inches (17.8 cm.). Although wine measures were advertised by colonial pewterers, none has survived, and even nineteenth-century examples are extremely scarce. This lidless, baluster-shaped measure is therefore not only desirable as a rare form but as a marked example of the work of the well-known pewterers Boardman and Hart.
Gift of Clara Lloyd-Smith Weber, 1979 (1979.449)

CERAMICS

233

Fig. 355. Detail, vase from the Rookwood Pottery Company, see Fig. 370.

The Colonial and Federal Periods, 1630–1830

356

Clays that could be used for making various types of pottery were plentiful in colonial America, as of course was wood to fire the potters' kilns. Consequently, ceramics were made to serve local needs from the earliest days of colonial settlement. Then and for many years to come, not only bricks, but roof tiles and kitchen, dairy, and table equipment were made of coarse red earthenware. These were simple, utilitarian forms that were usually washed or splashed with protective and sometimes decorative glazes of various colors.

These practical wares were made in many places, with some regional differences in form and decoration. Outstanding was the highly distinctive pottery of the Pennsylvania Germans, with colorful, sprightly designs and inscriptions. A wide variety of forms were made, from pitchers, jugs, plates, and mugs to flowerpots, shaving basins, and toy whistles. Two basic decorative techniques were employed: slip decoration and sgraffito. Both methods were centuries old and both were practiced in other areas of the country. Slip decoration was achieved by drawing with colored liquid clay, or "slip," on the pottery with a goose quill before the final firing (Fig. 356). Sgraffito designs were scratched through a slip coating with a stick, revealing the red-clay base beneath (Figs. 357 and 358). Graphic motifs and inscriptions were commonly taken from folk images and folklore carried over from the Old World to the New.

Stoneware, made of finer and denser clays that were fired at a much higher temperature than ordinary earthenware, was produced as early as the eighteenth century. The harder body of this ware could be glazed merely by throw-

Fig. 356. Covered jar, *North Carolina, 1785–1830; red earthenware, height 12¾ inches (32.4 cm.). This engaging form is known as a sugar jar in North Carolina, where the Moravians produced many of them from before the middle of the eighteenth century onward. Upon their arrival in America from Germany or Switzerland, most of the Moravians who eventually* *came to North Carolina lived for a time in Pennsylvania. Their pottery is different from what evolved in Pennsylvania, however, and this jar, decorated simply with bright stripes of slip, contrasts markedly with the Pennsylvania German sgraffito plate opposite.*
Rogers Fund, 1918 (18.95.16)

Fig. 357. Plate, *possibly by Henry Roudebuth (active about 1790–1816), Pennsylvania, about 1793; red earthenware, diameter 12¼ inches (31.1 cm.). Pennsylvania German pottery is characterized by bright colors and freely and humorously drawn flowers, birds, human figures, and animals—all of which set it apart from New England work. Here a sgraffito peacock struts across a yellow ground toward a tulip-like flower almost as big as he is—both motifs were popular in Pennsylvania German art. The cartouche containing the date 1793 and the initials H. R. is unusual and has led students—cautiously, in the absence of any supporting evidence—to entertain the thought that its maker may have been Henry Roudebuth of Montgomery County. Decorative plates like this were made not to use every day but to give as gifts or to mark special occasions.*
Gift of Mrs. Robert W. de Forest, 1933 (34.100.124)

357

Fig. 358. Tea canister, *Pennsylvania, about 1769; red earthenware, height 7½ inches (19 cm.). Besides being one of the earliest pieces of American pottery known, this is an unusual form both for earthenware and for Pennsylvania work. Canisters were nearly always part of tea sets made of much more elegant imported potteries and porcelains. Smaller and more gracefully proportioned, an English salt-glazed tea canister, from which this and two other similar examples were no doubt copied, would have had molded decoration in the form of a tea plant. Here a large tree bearing outsize fruit and supporting substantial scissor-tail birds has been scratched onto the canister to create a sgraffito surface very different from the suave, molded salt-glazed pro-*totype. *The names Joseph, Sally, and Smith and the date 1769 are scratched onto the surface, and the piece has thus been attributed to the Joseph Smith pottery of Bucks County, Pennsylvania.*

Purchase, Peter H. B. Frelinghuysen and Anonymous Gifts, and Friends of the American Wing Fund, 1981 (1981.46)

358

359

ing salt into the kiln when the fire was at its hottest. The result was a thin, colorless, very hard coating that was impervious to liquids. It was also resistant to acids, so that salt-glazed stoneware was popular for containers for vinegar, pickles, preserves, and the like. The practical advantages of this type of ware were obvious, and it was produced in various regions of the country throughout the nineteenth century.

Most stoneware was gray with decoration painted freehand in cobalt blue. One jug bears the incised inscription "Iohn Havins. 1775, July 18, N. York" and the mark "I. C.," probably the initials of the potter John Crolius of New York City (Fig. 359). The Crolius family was established in New York in the 1720s and, with the Remmey clan, dominated stoneware production there for most of the eighteenth century. In 1797, however, a pottery was established near Corlear's Hook on the East River near Grand Street, and until 1819 the stonewares made there competed successfully with those of the older potteries. The pleasingly formed and decorated jar shown here (Fig. 360) is one of numerous surviving examples that are stamped "Coerlear's Hook."

360

Fig. 359. Jug, *probably by John Crolius (1733–1812), 1775; stoneware, height 10 inches (25.4 cm.). Made of gray clay and decorated with incised scrolls colored blue, as was usual with such stonewares, this jug is most unusual in bearing the name of its owner, the initials of its maker, and the date and place of its manufacture. It is extremely rare to find stoneware of such an early date and with such complete documentation. During the eighteenth century, fear of the "infamously bad and unwholesome" lead glazes used* on common redware led to the widespread promotion of stoneware as a substitute, especially for the storage of acidic foods, which become poisonous when combined with lead. As a result, stoneware crocks and jugs were made in large numbers. Rogers Fund, 1934 (34.149)

Fig. 360. Jar, *probably by Thomas Commeraw (active 1797–1819) or David Morgan (active 1797–1802), New York, 1797–1819; stoneware, height 9½ inches (24.1 cm.). The smoothly* incised flower-and-leaf design colored with a deep cobalt blue glaze is typical of decorations on the wares produced by the pottery established late in the eighteenth century at Corlear's Hook on the East River in downtown Manhattan. Openmouthed jars of this kind were produced in quantity for use in the kitchen or pantry as storage receptacles for such diverse foods as preserves, cream, and butter. This example bears the incised identification "Coerlears Hook N. York." Rogers Fund, 1918 (18.95.13)

Fig. 361. Pitcher, by the American China Manufactory (1826–38), established by William Ellis Tucker (1800–32), Philadelphia, 1826–38; porcelain, height 9¼ inches (23.5 cm.). Fashionable European porcelains provided the inspiration for nearly all the decorative objects and tablewares William Ellis Tucker produced at his Philadelphia porcelain works, but this pitcher is an example of the one new form Tucker evolved. Its compact rounded body, high loop handle, and fluted base, although certainly expressive of the late neoclassical period in general, combine in a way that has not been found in pitchers from any other factory. Tucker's venture was short-lived, but while it lasted it was the first successful porcelain manufactory in the United States.

Purchase, Mrs. Russell Sage Gift, 1970 (1970.112)

361

The Pre-Centennial Period 1830–75

362

One of the most extensively produced types of pottery from about 1840 was a more pretentious earthenware that was mottled or streaked with a lustrous brown glaze often resembling tortoiseshell. It was known as Rockingham because pottery so glazed was first made in the eighteenth century at Swinton, England, on the estate of the Marquis of Rockingham. This and some other new types of pottery were shaped in molds rather than thrown on the wheel. The technique, like that of pressing glass, shifted the emphasis from the craftsman to the designer of molds and opened the door to mass production. Rockingham ware was molded into a wide variety of forms: doorknobs, paperweights, cuspidors, picture frames, pudding bowls, lamp bases, pitchers, and decorative objects of different sorts. It was produced at a number of factories in New Jersey, Maryland, Vermont, and Ohio. The figure of a reclining doe before a hollow tree trunk (Fig. 362), attributed to designer Daniel Greatbach at Bennington, Vermont, is a representative example. The new technique lent itself to more elegant wares as well. A light and delicate effect was achieved by the American Pottery Company of Jersey City, New Jersey, in their white teapot with molded decoration of meandering stems and flowers (Fig. 363).

Short-lived attempts to produce true porcelain were undertaken as early as the eighteenth century, notably from 1770 to 1772 by Bonnin and Morris of Philadelphia. Only a rare few of their works have survived. It was in 1826 that William Ellis Tucker, also of Philadelphia, opened the first really successful porcelain factory in America. The enterprise closed in 1838, but in its brief period of production it produced thin,

363

Fig. 362. Figure of a doe, by Lyman, Fenton and Company (1849–58), Bennington, Vermont, 1849–58; earthenware, height 8½ inches (21.6 cm.). Like the famous Bennington poodles, this doe and a recumbent stag were made as a pair to be used as mantel ornaments. They were never produced in great quantities and are thus relatively rare today. The flint-enamel glaze that covers the doe was a kind of improved Rockingham glaze—mottled brown with blue, green, and yellow added. This lively surface, developed by Bennington's genius potter, Christopher Weber Fenton, and patented in 1849 as Fenton's Enamel, was used for all kinds of decorative and utilitarian wares produced at Bennington.
Rogers Fund, 1938 (38.125.2)

Fig. 363. Teapot, by the American Pottery Company, Jersey City, New Jersey, 1843–48; earthenware, height 3¾ inches (9.5 cm.). Until the second quarter of the nineteenth century European ceramics manufacturers dominated the American market for fine ceramics, and D. and J. Henderson's American Pottery Manufacturing Company was one of the first American potteries to compete successfully. The firm specialized in Staffordshire types, and among their borrowings was the technique of making pottery in molds instead of on the potter's wheel. This was such an efficient and economical method of fashioning objects with elaborate relief decoration that other potteries were quick to follow their lead. Like the Bennington doe, this charming white pottery teapot, which bears the rare mark of its maker, was produced in a mold. Its decoration of low-relief vines and flowers and its acorn finial were taken from the Rococo Revival vocabulary, which was becoming more and more popular in the 1840s, when the teapot was made.
Sansbury-Mills Fund, 1982 (1982.67.1a,b)

Fig. 364. Pitcher, *by Charles Cartlidge and Company (1848–56), Greenpoint (Brooklyn), New York, 1848–56; porcelain, height 8¹⁄₈ inches (20.6 cm.). A lapse of ten years occurred between the closing of the Tucker porcelain manufactory and the opening of Cartlidge's porcelain works. Beginning with buttons, the firm moved on to produce such novelties as cane heads and doorknobs and then wares like this presentation pitcher. The classicism and restraint of the Tucker pitcher have now given way to Rococo Revival naturalism: sprays of oak leaves complete with acorns have been molded onto the sides of the pitcher; the handle is molded into a knobby branch shape; and the spout is in the form of the head and neck of an eagle. Several such pitchers are known, each bearing a different inscription. Obviously the customer decided on the inscription, which was applied to the pitcher after the order was placed.*
Sansbury-Mills Fund, 1979 (1979.67)

364

365

white, translucent wares that competed with European imports.

Although with the help of immigrant French craftsmen and some backing from local associates, Tucker (in partnership at various times with various people) turned out some elaborate pieces, most of the firm's output consisted of relatively simple adaptations of fashionable French, German, and English designs. Among them are several pitchers painted with imaginary landscapes in sepia and polychrome and with floral decorations in natural colors (Fig. 361). The shapes of these pieces reflect the neoclassical spirit of the time.

In the decades after the Tucker factory closed new adventures in American porcelain were undertaken. Around the middle of the nineteenth century Charles Cartlidge and Company of Greenpoint, New York, was producing porcelain in a variety of forms. Fashions had changed since the Tucker days, and the Cartlidge output visibly departed from the classical spirit of the earlier wares. A case in point is a robust, somewhat squat pitcher covered with naturalistic relief decorations corresponding to Rococo Revival styles (Fig. 364).

Parian ware, a white, waxy porcelain developed in England for use in unglazed objects, was also introduced into this country around the middle of the last century. It was so named because of its resemblance to marble quarried on the Aegean island of Paros. Indeed, it

Fig. 365. Pitcher, by the United States Pottery Company, Bennington, Vermont, about 1853; Parian porcelain, height 8¼ inches (21 cm.). Christopher Weber Fenton, who introduced Fenton's Enamel (see Fig. 362), also introduced Parian ware, a hard, marble-like porcelain that is translucent and has a smooth unglazed surface. It had been developed in Europe for making statues that were much less expensive than stone ones. Fenton quickly found that he could make all sorts of objects in Parian, especially those with highly modeled surfaces like that of this pitcher, on which a landscape in relief showing a waterfall, rocks, and trees is supposed to represent Niagara Falls. The piece combines the romantic mid-century attitude toward nature in general,

the American fascination with its own natural wonders in particular, and the pervasive Victorian interest in oddities.
Gift of Dr. Charles W. Green, 1947 (47.90.15)

Fig. 366. Vase, by the Union Porcelain Works (1863–about 1920), Greenpoint (Brooklyn), New York, about 1876; porcelain, height 12¾ inches (32.4 cm.). The Centennial celebration in Philadelphia inspired American manufacturers of all the decorative arts to scale new heights. Among the most attractive and successful were the "Century Vases" designed by Karl Mueller of the Union Porcelain Works. These incorporated patriotic motifs drawn from American history and recorded recent technological achievements

and native plants and animals. This version bears a band, in biscuit (unglazed porcelain), with panels of low-relief historical scenes; just above, on a surface patterned with leaves from native trees, is a profile bust of George Washington; bison heads serve as handles; and more American flowers and birds are drawn on the inner and outer surfaces of the neck of the vase. In praising the Union Porcelain Works's display, the Crockery and Glass Journal, a contemporary publication, encouraged other potteries to follow their lead: "Let American manufacturers make their own designs and leave off copying foreign ones!"
Gift of Mr. and Mrs. Franklin M. Chace, 1969 (69.194.1)

366

proved a happy substitute for that stone when it was molded into statuettes that were sometimes described as "Parian marble." There is also a sculptural quality to the Niagara Falls pitcher (Fig. 365) made by the United States Pottery Company at Bennington, Vermont, in celebration of America's natural wonders. Unlikely as such a subject was, the resultant form, an extreme expression of the naturalistic rococo decoration favored at the time, was surprisingly effective. Color was often used in Parian ware: a smooth white design stands out in relief against a pitted ground of blue, pink, buff, or green. These pieces were made in molds but finished by hand.

The United States International Exhibition, known as the Centennial, provided an excellent showcase for the improved porcelains that had been developed since mid-century. The Union Porcelain Works of Greenpoint (Brooklyn), New York, showed its "Century Vase" (Fig. 366), designed for the occasion by the gifted German-born sculptor Karl Mueller. A version of this monumental piece in the Museum's collection displays a relief profile of George Washington and has bison heads for handles. Panels in a band around the base contain relief figures recalling various aspects of American history. Mueller was also responsible for an impressive pedestal of biscuit (unglazed) porcelain with neoclassical figures in white relief against an apricot-colored ground (Fig. 367).

Fig. 367. Pedestal, by the Union Porcelain Works (1863–about 1920), Greenpoint (Brooklyn), New York, about 1876; porcelain, height 42½ inches (108 cm.). Another display piece designed by Karl Mueller for the Union Porcelain Works to take to the Centennial was this pedestal made of pale apricot and white biscuit porcelain. Americans felt the confidence that prosperity and a century of achievement in many different fields had brought, and they identified themselves with the classical Greek and Roman civilizations, whose accomplishments they admired. Using a classical column form and the classical Greek story of Electra as the decorative theme, the designer allied Americans with both the practical and artistic achievements of those legendary ancient civilizations. A contemporary account describes the Union Porcelain Works display, in which two of these pedestals support two "Century Vases."
Purchase, Anonymous Gift, 1968 (68.99.1a–d)

367

374

Fig. 374. Cup and saucer, part of the dinner service seen in Fig. 375. Diameter of saucer 5³/₁₆ inches (12.6 cm.), diameter of cup 3⁷/₁₆ inches (8 cm.).
Gift of Mr. and Mrs. Roger G. Kennedy, 1978 (1978.501.14,16)

another. However, they had paved the way for the individual studio potteries of the years ahead.

One of the first to recognize that machines could be put to work in the service of art was Frank Lloyd Wright. As early as 1901 he had written that the duty of dominating the machine "is relentlessly marked out for the artist in this, the Machine Age." His ability to practice what he preached is clearly demonstrated in the china he designed for the Imperial Hotel in Tokyo, one of Wright's best-known commissions. Primary colors and one abstract form—the circle—are combined to create china that is as pleasing to look at as it is practical to stack and use (Figs. 374 and 375).

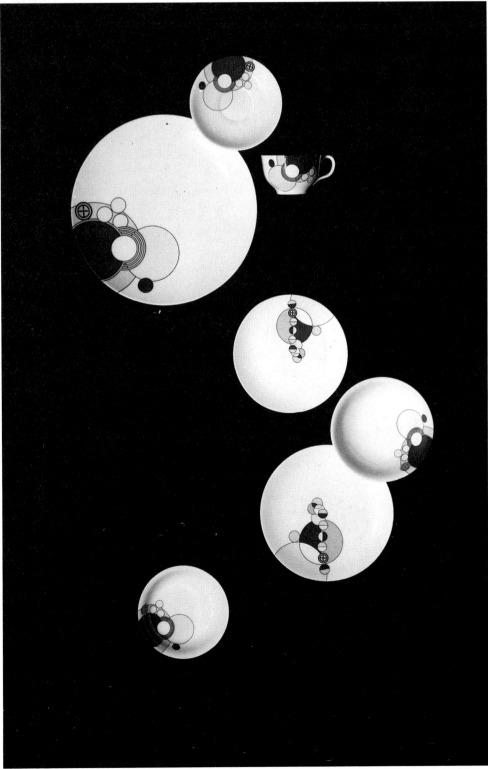

375

Fig. 375. Dinner service, by Frank Lloyd Wright (1867–1959), about 1922; porcelain, diameter of dinner plate 10⅝ inches (26.3 cm.). Frank Lloyd Wright was one of the first to realize that machines could be used to create honest, yet artistic, furnishings. As early as 1901 in his landmark lecture, "The Art and Craft of the Machine," delivered at Hull House in Chicago, Wright advanced his belief in mass production. These plates, bowls, and cups, which he designed for use at his great Imperial Hotel in Tokyo, prove that he was correct. In both form and ornament they make use of the circles that were to become an important element of Wright's designs for both buildings and furnishings, and they were easily produced by machine in whatever numbers were necessary.
Gift of Mr. and Mrs. Roger G. Kennedy, 1978 (1978.501.14,16,4,8,10,6,12)

GLASS

Fig. 376. *Detail, decanter from the Boston and Sandwich Glass Company, see Fig. 399.*

The Colonial and Federal Periods 1630–1830

Of the many materials used in the decorative arts, glass lends itself to the greatest variety of treatment. It can be freely blown and tooled to any conceivable form; it can be fashioned into a film of gossamer thinness or a solid of weighty bulk; it can be blown or pressed into patterned molds of many different shapes; it can be cut and engraved into glittering textures; it can be given gemlike colors that range the spectrum or endowed with crystalline clarity; it can be enameled with colorful designs. Over the past two centuries American glassmakers have taken advantage of all these possibilities.

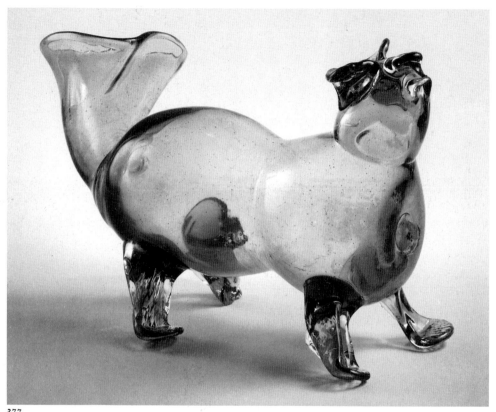

377

Glassmakers were included among the earliest immigrants, from Jamestown on, but the craft achieved a significant output only when the eighteenth century was well advanced and when artisans, Germans for the most part, established furnaces in several different colonies. Among the more enduring of these was the factory Caspar Wistar established in 1739 near Alloway in southern New Jersey with the aid of craftsmen brought to America from the Continent. German influence is clearly evident in the glassware produced by this factory, which operated for about forty years. Here, as at most American glasshouses until well into the nineteenth century, the commercial product consisted primarily of green ("common") glass bottles and windowpanes.

Wistar's factory also produced amusing decorative pieces and simple tablewares such as vases, bowls, sugar bowls, and pitchers. A frisky green-glass *Schnapshunde*, or bottle in the shape of a dog, attributed to Wistar (Fig. 377) is the sort of informal, or "offhand," piece that collectors seek. It has the charm that results from a glassblower's turning his skill to the pleasant task of creating amusing or useful objects for family and friends, having no reason to stick to conventional or predictable paths.

During the dozen years before the Revolution the Pennsylvania glasshouses of the fabulous "Baron" Henry William Stiegel, another German entrepreneur, advertised products as good as any imported from abroad. The pattern-molded sugar bowls, creamers,

408

Fig. 409. "Welcome" window, by John La Farge (1835–1910), New York, 1909; stained glass, 13 by 8 feet (4 by 2.4 m.). In the last two decades of the nineteenth century when art glass was at its most popular, with its emphasis on brilliant and unusual color effects, stained-glass windows were incorporated into many "artistic" houses. La Farge, who was internationally acclaimed for his contributions to the art of stained glass, made this richly colored window for the home of Mrs. George T. Bliss at 9 East Sixty-eighth Street in New York. In it he made use of his "American glass"—opaque, translucent, iridescent, and very much in keeping with the opulent interior his window graced.
Gift of Susan Dwight Bliss, 1944 (44.90)

of the century, and they are today eagerly sought by those who can afford the very high prices that examples command—when they can be found.

Like Tiffany, the artist-designer-craftsman John La Farge used stained glass to create deeply and richly colored paintings in glass (Fig. 409). Like Tiffany too, La Farge was famous both at home and abroad as a pioneer practitioner of the art of stained glass. The rich hues that both men worked so hard to achieve—adding layer after layer to arrive at just the right texture and tone—contrasted markedly with the simpler colored and stained glasses that architects George Elmslie and Frank Lloyd Wright used in their windows. Choosing much lighter shades and neatly delineated shapes, they created leaded-glass windows whose abstract patterns repeated and reinforced the lines of the houses for which the windows were designed (Fig. 410). As Elmslie wrote of his own work in *Western Architect* for January 1913: "It is all intensely organic, proceeding from main motif to minor motifs, interrelating and to the last terminal, all of a piece. . . ."

Wright's most successful stained-glass windows were those made in 1912 for the Avery Coonley playhouse (see Fig. 4, really a kindergarten run by Mrs. Coonley). Wright had completed the Coonley residence at Riverside, Illinois, a few years earlier and thought it was the best work he had done up to that time. Here all reference to the naturalistic themes and tints typical of so much of Tiffany's glass have given way to abstract, geometric patterns ultimately based on the shapes of things children play with at parties—balloons, flags, and confetti—expressed almost starkly in primary colors. Wright dubbed the

410

triptych window a "kinder-symphony," but its abstract design also inevitably recalls the nonobjective experiments with paint and canvas that were being undertaken about the same time by the avant-garde Dutch painter Piet Mondrian.

Fig. 410. Window, by George Grant Elmslie (1871–1953) of Purcell, Feick and Elmslie (1909–13), Minneapolis, 1911; clear and stained leaded glass, height 60 inches (152.4 cm.). The Arts and Crafts approach to stained glass was of course very different from that of Beaux-Arts and Art Nouveau designers such as La Farge and Tiffany. Like Wright (see Fig 4), Elmslie used colored-glass windows in severely stylized and geometric patterns composed of clear glass combined with stained glass in cool, light colors. The window shown here is from the stair hall of the J. C. Cross house in Minneapolis, which Elmslie's firm remodeled in 1911.
Gift of Roger G. Kennedy, 1972 (1972.20.2)

426

Fig. 426. Thomas Jefferson (detail), by John Trumbull (1765–1843), about 1788; oil on wood, 4½ by 3¼ inches (11.4 by 8.3 cm.). When the two men were in Paris in 1786, Trumbull first painted Jefferson's portrait to include in his best-known work, The Declaration of Independence. Later, Trumbull painted three small modified versions of that portrait, of which this is one. It was owned originally by Jefferson's good friend Angelica Church, who wrote him in 1788 that their mutual friend Maria Cosway's similar portrait (now at Yale) ". . . is a better likeness than mine, but then I have a better elsewhere and so I console myself."
Bequest of Cornelia Cruger, 1924 (24.19.1)

427

427), painted in 1789 when he was in London, does not relate to American history, but depicts an episode during the three-year siege of the English fortress by French and Spanish forces. In 1781 General George Elliot led a nighttime foray during which the British destroyed an entire line of the enemy's counterworks. Trumbull chose to dramatize the moment when the gallant Spaniard Don José de Barboza, although mortally wounded, refused British help because that would have meant complete surrender to the

Fig. 427. The Sortie Made by the Garrison at Gibraltar, by John Trumbull (1765–1843), 1789; oil on canvas, 70½ by 106 inches (179.1 by 269.2 cm.). Instead of focusing on the momentous events that had recently taken place in his own country, Trumbull chose, in this eminently successful history painting, to show an episode at Gibraltar in which the British defeated a Spanish attempt to take over their garrison. At center is a Spanish officer fatally wounded in the encounter, but refusing help from the British, who are portrayed as dignified and magnanimous in victory. Trumbull was criticized by his countrymen for portraying the British in a heroic light when they had so recently been at war with America, but he replied that nobility and heroism,

wherever they were found, were worthy subjects. He further explained in his autobiography: "I was pleased with the subject, as offering, in the gallant conduct and death of the Spanish commander, a scene of deep interest to the feelings, and in the contrast of the darkness of night, with the illumination of an extensive conflagration, great splendor of effect and color."
Purchase, Pauline V. Fullerton Bequest, Mr. and Mrs. Walter Carter Gift, Mr. and Mrs. Raymond J. Horowitz Gift, Erving Wolf Foundation Gift, Vain and Harry Fish Foundation, Inc. Gift, Gift of Hanson K. Corning, by exchange, and Maria DeWitt Jesup and Morris K. Jesup Funds, 1976 (1976.332)

Fig. 428. George Washington, *by Gilbert Stuart (1755–1828), about 1795; oil on canvas, 30¼ by 25¼ inches (76.8 by 64.1 cm.). Stuart returned to America in 1793 after years of living abroad, and soon found a market for his portraits, which were far better than those of any of his American contemporaries. Likenesses of George Washington shortly became his stock in trade, and this, named the Gibbs-Channing-Avery portrait after its former owners, is considered one of the best versions. It is modeled on his first Washington portrait, called the Vaughan Washington, after Washington's good friend Samuel Vaughan, who commissioned it in 1795. That portrait was so well received that Stuart was* deluged with requests for copies, of which this is one. Because this portrait is remarkably lifelike, with vivid facial color and a calm, penetrating gaze, it is thought that Stuart painted some of it, at least, from life.
Rogers Fund, 1907 (07.160)

Fig. 429. An Osage Warrior *(detail), by Charles Balthazar-Julien Fevret de Saint-Mémin (1770–1852), about 1804; watercolor, 7¼ by 6⁵⁄₁₆ inches (18.4 by 16 cm.). Although this watercolor portrait is small, it is very impressive, stressing the warrior's strength and dignity through his bold profile and steadfast expression. His blanket-like wrap, distinctive native hair treatment, and jewelry add color and character to a likeness dominated by monumental impassivity.*
The Elisha Whittlesey Collection, The Elisha Whittlesey Fund, 1954 (54.82)

428

enemy. Trumbull explained his choice of a British, rather than an American, subject: "to show that noble and generous actions, by whomsoever performed, were the objects to whose celebration I meant to devote myself."

Most of West's numerous American pupils returned home with developed skills that established fresh standards in post-Revolutionary American art. One of the most celebrated of these repatriates was the witty, urbane, and bibulous Gilbert Stuart, who mastered a highly distinctive style of portraiture that earned him considerable prestige in England and attracted wide patronage in the new republic. Omitting accessory paraphernalia of the kind that inform and enlighten Copley's paintings, Stuart reduced detail to a minimum in his portraits, often skimping even on bodies and backgrounds. One early critic remarked that Stuart could not, in fact, paint "below the fifth button"; Stuart himself said that he left such accessories to the tailor. "He paints very fast," observed one Russian visitor to the United States about 1812, "and his portraits are more like excellent sketches than like completed paintings."

Stuart claimed that he returned to America to paint a portrait of George Washington, although one of the compelling reasons for his leaving the British Isles was to avoid the very real horrors of the debtors' prison to which his gross extravagance had made him vulnerable.

Of the innumerable portraits of Washington he did produce, the Museum has, among others, a fine early example that represents Stuart's classical American style in its pure form (Fig. 428). Apparently done in part from life, this canvas, the Gibbs-Channing-Avery Washington, is known by the names of its former owners. So well known have such likenesses of the first president become that if he should return to earth he would have to resemble Stuart's portraits to be recognized.

An even more archetypal American than George Washington is seen in Fig. 429—*An Osage Warrior.* The portraitist, Charles Balthazar-Julien Fevret de Saint-Mémin, was a Frenchman who worked in America from the 1790s to 1814, when he returned to France permanently. He is well known for his more than 800 American portraits produced by means of a physionotrace—an instrument invented in 1786 by Gilles Louis Chrétien and improved by Saint-Mémin—that enabled him to record the exact outline of his subject's profile in all its minute details.

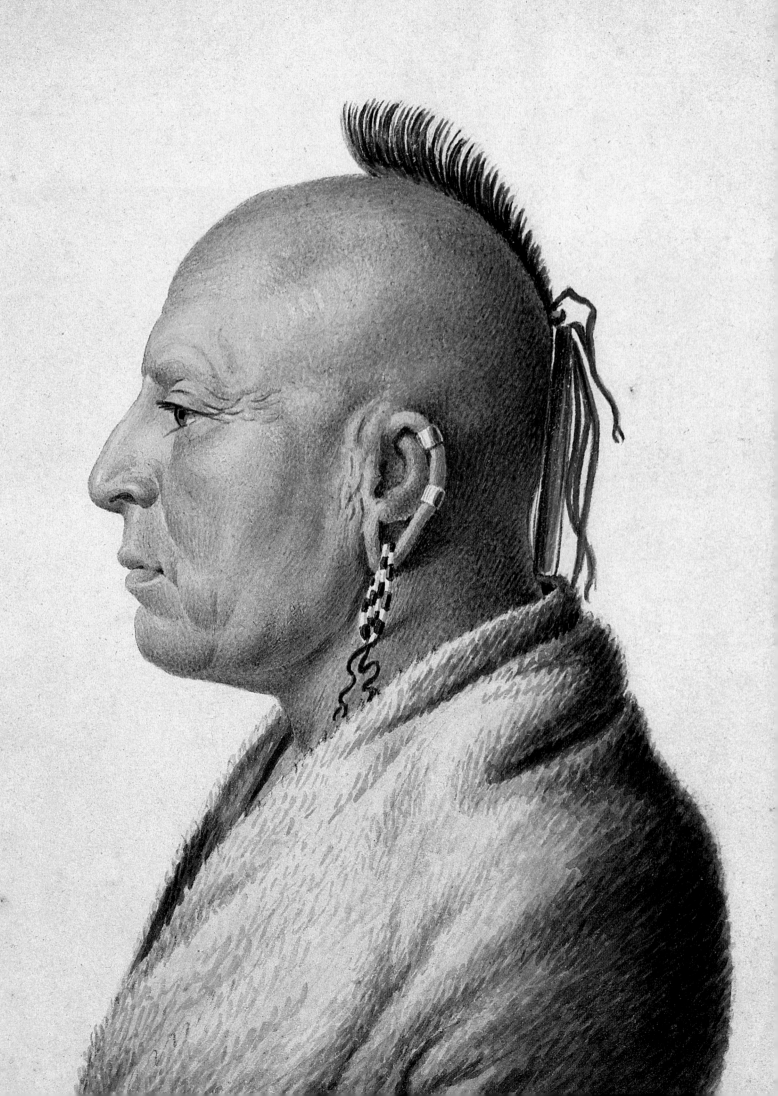

430

431

432

Figs. 430–37. Miniatures. *The art of painting miniatures was practiced in the colonies from the early decades of the eighteenth century. Over the years many artists best known for their oil paintings on canvas were attracted to this very exacting medium—among them Copley, Charles Willson Peale, and Trumbull. Others specialized in the particular art of painting "in little." Miniature paintings are delicate and fragile, and for this reason, as in the case of watercolors, they cannot long be exposed to strong light without risk.*

433

Fig. 430. Robert Macomb, *by Edward Greene Malbone (1783–1832), about 1806; watercolor on ivory, 3¾ inches by 3 inches (9.5 by 7.6 cm.).* Bequest of Irving S. Olds, 1963 (63.122.1)

Fig. 431. George Washington, *by John Ramage (about 1748–1802), 1796; watercolor on ivory, 2¹/₁₆ by 1³/₈ inches (5.2 by 3.5 cm.).* Bequest of Charles Allen Munn, 1924 (24.109.93)

Fig. 432. The Thompson Children, *by John Carlin (1813–91), 1846; watercolor on ivory, 4¹/₈ by 3¹/₃ inches (10.5 by 8.6 cm.).* Morris K. Jesup and Maria DeWitt Jesup Funds, 1979 (1979.188)

Fig. 433. Gilbert Stuart, *by Sarah Goodridge (1788–1853), about 1825; watercolor on ivory, 3¹/₄ by 2¹/₂ inches (8.3 by 6.4 cm.).* Gift of Misses Sarah and Josephine Lazarus, 1888–95 (95.14.123)

Fig. 434. Jeremiah Lee, *by John Singleton Copley (1738–1815), 1769; watercolor on ivory, 1¹/₂ by 1¹/₄ inches (3.8 by 3.2 cm.).* Harris Brisbane Dick Fund, 1939 (39.174)

Fig. 435. Lieutenant Alexander Murray, *by James Peale (1749–1831), about 1780; watercolor on ivory, 2¹/₂ by 1¹⁵/₁₆ inches (6.4 by 4.9 cm.).* Rogers Fund, 1925 (25.29)

Fig. 436. Miss Ross, *by James Peale (1749–1831), 1791; watercolor on ivory, 2 by 1⁹/₁₆ inches (5.1 by 4 cm.).* Fletcher Fund, 1941 (41.36)

Fig. 437. Portraits of the Artist's Children, *by Thomas Seir Cummings (1804–94), about 1841; watercolor on ivory, length 17¹/₂ inches (44.5 cm.).* Gift of Mrs. Richard B. Hartshorne and Miss Fanny S. Cummings, 1928 (28.148.1–9)

437

A meticulous technique was required to produce these works, many American examples of which, among the best in the world at the time, were painted on ivory especially prepared by stippling or crosshatching. This provided a surface texture that could receive a tiny painted image without so much as a pinhead's area of flaw in the exquisitely thin brushstrokes that were required. There was no room for even a very small mistake in creating the final image and practically none for making corrections after the first washes of color had been laid on the ivory. As in

Homer's watercolors, where the unpainted white surfaces of the paper often served as highlights, so in the case of miniatures the unbleached and undisguised ivory served the same purpose. It provided as well an underlying glow for the thin, transparent coverings of color in other areas. In scrutinizing these works at close range, as must be done to appreciate their special qualities, it is almost literally necessary to hold one's breath for a moment—as indeed the artist probably had to do to create them.

Miniatures are intimate personal documents,

intended to serve as an evocative reminder of a cherished friend, relative, or admirer. Not infrequently the emotional attachment suggested by the precious little work was intensified by a lock of the sitter's hair or a fragment of a written message set in the back of a gold or silver frame. The result had an almost talismanic quality of recalling a distant presence or revivifying a departed soul in fond remembrance.

434

435

436

The Early Nineteenth Century, 1790–1840

438

Figs. 438 and 439. Lady with Her Pets, *by Rufus Hathaway (1770–1822), 1790; oil on canvas, 34¼ by 32 inches (87 by 81.3 cm.). One of the most strikingly decorative of all American naïve, or folk, portraits, and one of the most successful in terms of composition and characterization, this is Hathaway's earliest known work. The subject is said to be Molly Whales Leonard of Marshfield, Massachusetts, and much of her charm derives from the descriptive details Hathaway included—her feathered headdress, painted fan, and Chippendale chair. While all these establish Mrs. Leonard as a distinctive character, her "pets" add even more to her individuality.*

There are two birds, one perched beside her on the crest of the chair and one a parrot in a hoop; two butterflies; and a cat beside whom is lettered the word "Canter," which is perhaps his name. The crackled surface of the painting, which is as much a distinguishing feature as anything else, is thought to be the result of Hathaway's improper combination of materials. The engaging Mrs. Leonard remains in her original frame, which is painted in black and ivory to simulate marble.
Gift of Edgar William and Bernice Chrysler Garbisch, 1963 (63.201.1)

"The signing of the Declaration of Independence in 1776," wrote folk-art authority Jean Lipman, "also signaled the beginning of a new independence for American art. The seeds of the native folk tradition, planted with the founding of the American colonies in the seventeenth century, sprouted and throve all along the eastern seaboard from the last quarter of the eighteenth century through the first three quarters of the nineteenth." And it wasn't only folk art that flourished after the Revolution—it was art of all kinds. West, Copley, and Trumbull were followed to Europe at first by scores and then by hundreds of aspiring American artists seeking instruction in the European academic tradition. Although many European-trained artists were eventually successful at home, several of the leading members of this first generation of formally trained painters were out of tune with their countrymen, and their work went unappreciated. Folk artists, on the other hand, were not concerned with the high ideals that burdened their academic brethren. Their sometimes crazily drawn but always frank images of people, animals, and scenes both real and imaginary usually appealed as much to their clients as they do to the swelling ranks of modern folk-art collectors.

"American folk art" is a term that is loosely used to cover a wide range of paintings, sculptures, and artifacts of various descriptions. Sometimes this highly miscellaneous category is alternatively known as primitive art, naïve art, or the art of the common man. By whatever name, the material referred to is typically the output of men and women who, to the best of their abilities, adapted their innate skills to the needs,

Above, below, where'er the astonished eye
Turns to behold, new opening wonders lie,

With uproar hideous first the *Falls* appear,
The stunning tumult thundering on the ear.

This great overwhelming work of awful Time
In all its dread magnificence sublime,

Rises on our view, amid a crashing roar
That bids us kneel, and Time's great God adore.

The Falls   *of Niagara*

18   25

440

441

circumstances, and possibilities of their daily lives.

While much folk art remains anonymous, the identity of many practitioners has been disclosed through diligent work by students and collectors. *Lady with Her Pets* (Figs. 438 and 439), inscribed "RH Octr 1790," can be ascribed to one Rufus Hathaway of Massachusetts, who late in the eighteenth century became the town doctor of Duxbury. When he was not engaged in medical pursuits, Hathaway painted portraits, including miniatures, at least one landscape and a still life, and also apparently made picture frames and wood carvings. Whether the feathered bonnet and other costume accessories were the lady's own possessions, studio props, or inventions used to offset the rigid posture and angular face and to create a pleasing pattern, remains conjectural.

A double portrait of *Edward and Sarah Rutter* (Fig. 441), the children of Captain Joshua Rutter of Baltimore, was painted about 1805 by Joshua Johnston (or Johnson), the earliest black artist known to have practiced in this country. More than a score of his portraits have been identified. As here, most of them are characterized by a subtle use of bright color and elegant detail. The Rutter children are shown dressed in their Sunday best for this important occasion, when their likenesses were recorded for the lasting pleasure of their proud parents—and as it turned out, of posterity. Johnston's customary style suggests that he may have been influenced by the work of Charles Peale Polk, a nephew of Charles Willson Peale, who was active in Baltimore during the 1790s.

Although he referred to himself as a "poor, illiterate mechanic," Edward Hicks remains one of the best known and most engaging of American folk artists. He was a cantankerous spirit who once confessed to his diary that his "poor zig-zag nature" predisposed him to extremes. But he succeeded in reconciling his intense religiosity with his artistic proclivities. His favorite theme was the peaceable kingdom, illustrating Isaiah's prophecy of a world at peace under the reign of the Messiah: "The wolf also shall dwell with the lamb, and the leopard shall lie down with the kid; and the calf and the young lion and the fatling together; and a little child shall

Fig. 441. **Edward and Sarah Rutter,** *by Joshua Johnston (or Johnson, active 1789–1824), about 1805; oil on canvas, 36 by 32 inches (91.4 by 81.3 cm.). Edward Pennington and Sarah Ann were the children of Captain Joshua Rutter of Baltimore, and Johnston has shown them dressed in their Sunday best, regarding us solemnly. Like Hathaway, Johnston painted his subjects' pet bird, and he also placed a colorful cluster of strawberries in Sarah's hand. Johnston is the first black portrait painter known to have worked in America—twenty-two unsigned and undated portraits have been attributed to him.*
Gift of Edgar William and Bernice Chrysler Garbisch, 1965 (65.254.3)

Fig. 442. **Mrs. Mayer and Her Daughter,** *by Ammi Phillips (1788–1865), 1830–40; oil on canvas, 37⅞ by 34¼ inches (96.2 by 87 cm.). Foremost among American painters of the flat, two-dimensional likenesses known as folk portraits was Ammi Phillips, who traveled about rural New York, Connecticut, and Massachusetts painting friends, relatives, and friends of friends from about 1811 to the 1860s. It is not the likenesses that we admire today, for they were remote at best; it is the design—the rhythms and masses—of the composition. In this portrait, painted during the middle of his career, Phillips provides drama and interest through large, simply shaped masses. The faces of Mrs. Mayer*

and her child, and her lacy cap, serve as bright counterpoints in an otherwise somber composition.
Gift of Edgar William and Bernice Chrysler Garbisch, 1962 (62.256.2)

442

443

Fig. 443. Tavern sign, United States, 1800–10; white pine, painted, 60 by 41 inches (152.4 by 104.1 cm.). Taverns were important in early America not just as providers of food and lodging to travelers, but to local citizens as centers for exchanging news and gossip and for doing business. The same itinerant painters who produced portraits, decorated houses, or enlivened coaches painted tavern signs—one of the earliest forms of commercial advertising. This example, depicting a scrawny rooster perched on a docile lion, probably symbolizes the victory of the colonies (the rooster crowing "Liberty") over England (the defeated lion), as well as informing weary travelers that food, drink, and a clean bed were finally at hand.
Gift of Mrs. Russell Sage, 1909 (10.125.404)

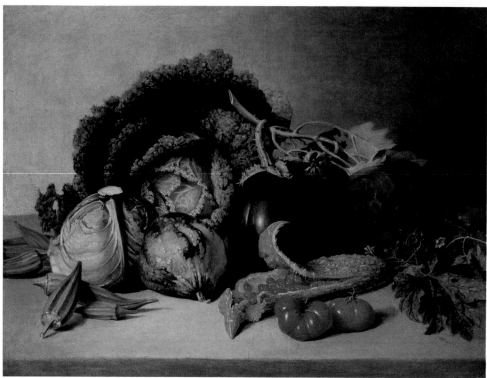

444

Fig. 444. **Still Life: Balsam Apple and Vegetables,** by James Peale (1749–1831), probably 1820s; oil on canvas, 20¼ by 26½ inches (51.4 by 67.3 cm.). Although American artists were interested in still life in the eighteenth century, they didn't devote themselves to it until the nineteenth. James and Raphaelle Peale (Charles Willson's brother and eldest son, respectively) led in developing a Philadelphia school of still life. This example, which presents a tempting, colorful assortment of vegetables, including a balsam apple, is a masterpiece of the genre, with a strong and satisfying pyramidal composition and direct, clear illumination.
Maria DeWitt Jesup Fund, 1939 (39.52)

lead them." Nearly 100 variant versions of this subject, preachments in paint, have survived.

Left an orphan at a tender age, Hicks was raised by a Quaker family, and in time, after a period of relatively free living, he became a dedicated preacher of that faith, for which he received no remuneration. He had early apprenticed himself to a carriage maker, taught himself to paint, and spent most of his life in Newtown, Pennsylvania, making and decorating coaches, designing signs and mileposts, and painting landscapes, including views of his neighbors' farms, and biblical allegories. However, he occasionally traveled many miles on horseback, sometimes in the dead of winter, which for some reason he thought might improve the condition of his ailing lungs. On one of these arduous journeys he visited Niagara Falls. He recorded that visit with a painting of the scene whose composition he copied from a vignette on a map by an earlier artist (Fig. 440). To this he added a decorative border combining verses from the poem "The Foresters" by ornithologist and explorer Alexander Wilson.

Ammi Phillips is another artist who has been rediscovered in fairly recent times. For fifty years this itinerant portraitist worked what was once known as the border country, a limited region of the Berkshires that included New York, Connecticut, and Massachusetts. Over that long period his style varied, as can be told from the hundreds of likenesses attributed to his brush. Phillips would paint portraits of each member of a household, then move on to do the same at the household of a related family in a nearby town. In 1825 the artist John Vanderlyn wrote a letter encouraging his nephew to become a portrait

Fig. 445. **Ariadne,** *by Asher B. Durand (1796–1886), after John Vanderlyn, 1835; engraving, 17½ by 20¾ inches (44.5 by 52.7 cm.). Although, artistically speaking, this subject was Vanderlyn's most successful, it failed to arouse any interest among the American public. Durand admired it very much; he bought it, copied it in oil, and then engraved it. This time the public responded positively, bringing fame to* Ariadne *and greater renown to Durand, who was already America's foremost engraver. Even so, Durand preferred painting to engraving, and the* New York Mirror *noted in 1836 that "Mr. Durand has almost relinquished the graver. Perhaps he thinks he cannot go beyond his* Ariadne. *No one else can."*
Gift of Samuel P. Avery, 1897 (97.29.2)

445

painter. "Indeed," Vanderlyn observed, "moving about the country as Phillips did and probably still does, must be an agreeable way of passing one's time." *Mrs. Mayer and Her Daughter* represents one phase of his sizable output (Fig. 442).

For almost a century, one member or another of the extraordinary family headed by Charles Willson Peale was painting pictures. In the 1820s, when he was in his seventies, Charles Willson's brother James Peale, who also had served in the Revolutionary army, produced *Balsam Apple and Vegetables* (Fig. 444). In this remarkably convincing still life the varied shapes, textures, colors, and all but the very taste of cabbage, eggplant, okra, tomatoes, and the balsam apple are presented in an opulent composition.

In the years following the War of 1812, the scene had shifted to a generation of artists who were too young to remember the Revolution and who, for the most part, had the advantage of solid professional training. It was these painters who sowed the seeds of romanticism that eventually found fertile ground in America and produced a wide and varied flowering of talent as the nation spread across the continent. The high level of competence of these men is demonstrated in the canvases of Washington Allston, John Vanderlyn, Samuel F. B. Morse, Thomas Sully, Charles C. Ingham, George P. A. Healy, and a score of others whose work is represented in the Museum's collection.

John Vanderlyn was the first American painter to look to France rather than to England for professional experience. He was the protégé of Aaron Burr, who sent him to Philadelphia to study with Gilbert Stuart for a year and then, in 1796, when Vanderlyn was twenty-one years old, to Paris for further study. There he spent the next five years. After a brief return visit to the United States, he recrossed the Atlantic and went to Paris in the company of Washington Allston, who was to be his lifelong friend. Vanderlyn spent the best part of twenty years in Europe and won some distinction there: in 1808 Napoleon awarded one of his paintings a gold medal.

Back in America once again after his extended European stay, Vanderlyn undertook his most ambitious work, a panoramic view of the palace and gardens of Versailles (Figs. 446, 447, and 448). It is the largest and in some ways the most unusual painting that has ever been exhibited in the Museum. The subject, designed as a continuous circular panorama, covers almost 2,000 square feet of canvas. It is a spectacular tour de force contrived by an accomplished draftsman—though Vanderlyn employed assistants to help him complete this prodigious job. The perspective has been ingeniously adjusted to the circular shape so that the spectator standing at dead center finds convincing vistas leading off in all directions. Onto this deceptively real stage Vanderlyn has introduced a crowd of tourists colorfully clad for a holiday amid the splendors of the world's most famous palace.

The painting was originally planned for exhibition in the Rotunda (Fig. 449), a building at the northeast corner of New York's City Hall Park, erected by the artist with the financial help of his friends. City officials rented Vanderlyn the plot of land for one peppercorn a year. Although he never thought of the panorama as being in the same class with his less extravagant creations, Vanderlyn hoped that it would attract large crowds of paying visitors and that it would lead them to appreciate the "higher branches" of art. These were represented in neighboring galleries by paintings by Vanderlyn and some of his fellow artists. Neither objective was achieved to his satisfaction. One of his own paintings, "Ariadne asleep, naked and abandoned by Theseus," as he described it, was not approved by the public in this country. It was one of the earliest and perhaps the most successful nudes by an American artist of the neoclassical period, and it was finally sold for $600 to Vanderlyn's fellow artist Asher Durand, who made engraved copies that popularized the subject and marked the culmination of Durand's high reputation as an engraver (see Fig. 445). In the end Vanderlyn died alone, embittered, and reduced to virtual beggary in a rented tavern room.

While Vanderlyn concentrated on Europe, other artists were taking a close look at the common American man in his eastern habitats, both rural and village, and on the western rivers and plains, and were reporting him at work and play in a spirit of flattering candor. Hardly any aspect of daily life escaped their brushes—and daily life in America around mid-century was more richly varied than it had ever been before. In William Sidney Mount's quiet and genial pictures of his Long Island neighbors, as in his *Cider Making* (Fig. 450), completed in 1841 during the burgeoning days of democracy, there is an intimacy and at times a humor that reflect a bond between the artist and a broad public. *Raffling for the Goose* and *Long Island Farmhouses*, both in the Museum's collection along with numerous other

Figs. 446, 447, and 448. The Palace and Gardens of Versailles, *by John Vanderlyn (1775–1852), 1816–19; oil on canvas, 12 by 165 feet (3.6 by 50 m.). In a day when long-distance travel was much more arduous than it is today, panoramas showing distant and exotic parts of the world were popular. The scenes were painted on huge canvas strips that could be rolled up and taken about the countryside for the entertainment of the populace. Vanderlyn's panorama of Versailles is a unique survival from that period, for the rough and careless handling these canvases received as they were carted from city to city, and the damp, rodent- and insect-infested storage spaces they were consigned to, meant that most were eventually damaged beyond repair.*

Vanderlyn's hope, in offering his grand view of Europe's most magnificent palace, was that viewers would be impressed and inspired enough by this example of monumental artistic achievement to become interested in the art of their own country—and particularly in Vanderlyn's own portrait and history paintings, which hung in a gallery near the panorama. His hope was never realized, for Americans were not attracted by his ambitious, but rather sterile, formal view of Versailles. Although Vanderlyn later decided that his American audience would have preferred a panorama of New York, it may be that they simply wanted more detail—a livelier, richer depiction of the human scene in and about the palace. At any rate, in 1824 Vanderlyn wrote that "on the

whole the exhibition of this picture failed altogether in the success I anticipated. . . ." Apparently as a result, his whole career went steadily downhill, and he died impoverished and embittered.

Gift of the Senate House Association, Kingston, New York, 1952 (52.184)

446

447

deur of the American countryside. Its wildness—seen in the thick woods and stark dead tree of the foreground and in the ominous thunderclouds above them—provides a dramatic contrast to the tranquil atmosphere that prevails around the Oxbow. For Cole, this landscape held a message, which is well expressed in a poem he wrote the year before he painted it:

> I sigh not for a stormless clime,
> Where drowsy quiet ever dwells;
> Where crystal brooks, with endless chime,
> Flow winding through perennial dells.
>
> For storms bring beauty in their train. . . .

Gift of Mrs. Russell Sage, 1908 (08.228)

454

Fig. 454. **Luman Reed,** *by Asher B. Durand (1796–1886), about 1835; oil on canvas, 30⅛ by 25⅜ inches (76.5 by 64.5 cm.).* Luman Reed, wrote Asher Durand's son, was "the first wealthy and intelligent connoisseur who detected and encouraged native ability in other directions than portraiture." Besides Durand, Reed patronized and befriended Thomas Cole and William Sidney Mount and paid the European travel and study expenses of several other artists. His house contained a gallery on the top floor—the first such space designated by an American entirely for the display of pictures—and the public was admitted to view his collection one day a week.
Bequest of Mary Fuller Wilson, 1963 (63.36)

455

456

Fig. 455. The Beeches, *by Asher B. Durand (1796–1886), 1846; oil on canvas, 60⅜ by 48⅛ inches (153.4 by 122.2 cm.). At the beginning of his career, Durand was an engraver, becoming one of the most prominent in the country. Among his productions were engravings of views by Thomas Cole and other members of the Hudson River school, and in the 1830s Durand laid down his graver and joined his Hudson River friends as a full-time landscape painter. The need for meticulous observation and attention to detail necessary for superior engravings served Durand well in his paintings. In* The Beeches *the tree stumps and trunks, the leaves growing on and beneath the two trees in the foreground, and the light filtering down and casting shadows, are exceedingly realistically rendered.*
Bequest of Maria DeWitt Jesup, 1915 (15.30.59)

painting in the years surrounding the Civil War. In benign and intensely atmospheric works such as *Autumn Oaks* (Fig. 456), the largely self-taught Inness recorded the smiling aspects of the American countryside after the disasters of the war had passed from the scene. Inness's profoundly spiritual nature shaped his vision of the world about him. From the 1840s to the 1870s he made repeated visits to Europe, and these experiences influenced his artistic development. He was one of the first Americans to admire the work of the Barbizon painters in France, although he neither copied nor imitated any of them. His style was his own, and it changed as he matured.

A preoccupation with the effects of light and atmosphere characterized a sizable group of these later landscapists. In *The Coming Storm* (Fig. 457), Heade reveals an intense love of nature and of light, poetically stated. The two isolated figures and the single white sail under the threatening dark cloud produce an almost surrealistic impression typical of this artist's landscapes.

Fitz Hugh Lane was America's first native-born marine painter of real merit. His *Stage Fort Across Gloucester Harbor* (Fig. 458), recorded in subtle colors and with highly skilled draftsmanship, is characteristic of his serene and spacious views of the New England waterfront he knew so intimately. Lane was sensitive to the changing moods of sea and sky, and he thoroughly understood marine architecture. His work had a strong influence on younger painters of his day.

Kensett's *Lake George*, painted in 1869, is a subtle counterpoint of land,

Fig. 456. Autumn Oaks, *by George Inness (1824–94), about 1875; oil on canvas, 21⅛ by 30¼ inches (53.7 by 76.8 cm.). In this scene Inness celebrates both the calm and beauty of the countryside and autumn's glorious colors. By showing the sun streaming down on the flaming foliage in the foreground, Inness makes the color and the trees the dominant notes in his composition. Their brilliance is emphasized further by the deep shadows of the immediate foreground and the purple-gray clouds overhead.*
Gift of George I. Seney, 1887 (87.8.8)

Fig. 457. The Coming Storm, *by Martin Johnson Heade (1819–1904), 1859; oil on canvas, 28 by 44 inches (71.1 by 111.8 cm.). Like many other artists of his generation, Heade was fascinated by the ever-changing aspect of nature—by the atmospheric effects produced by an oncoming storm, for example. Here he captures the quiet period that often precedes a storm, when the water and air seem perfectly still. The motionless man and dog in the foreground emphasize nature's transient tranquility.*
Gift of Erving Wolf Foundation and Mr. and Mrs. Erving Wolf, 1975 (1975.160)

457

water, and shimmering atmosphere (Fig. 459). That much-painted lake has rarely if ever been pictured with the moving expressiveness that pervades Kensett's rendering of it. Like several other prominent artists of the post–Civil War period, Kensett became one of the founders of the Metropolitan Museum.

A very different but equally atmospheric marine subject is Nathaniel Currier's hand-colored lithograph *Clipper Ship "Red Jacket"* (Fig. 460). Produced in 1855, two years before Currier joined with James M. Ives, this print typifies the attitude that was to become standard for Currier and Ives in em-

phasizing American enterprise, accomplishment, and prosperity (Fig. 461). With a few exceptions, the problems and tragedies that accompanied urbanization, war, and massive influxes of immigrants were left to others to portray. At first Currier and Ives's black and white prints were hand colored by teams of women, usually working at home, but later chromolithography, in which several stones with identical images were superimposed in as many basic colors, mechanized the procedure of color reproduction. The firm thus produced untold numbers of inexpensive prints that all but flooded the nation, bringing fair approximations of paint-

ings to the attention of scores of thousands of Americans who had no other means of knowing the originals.

Currier and Ives, along with many of their contemporaries, helped to shape Americans' vision of themselves. Generations of Americans have formed visual impressions of our country's early days from sentimentalized representations of our life and history produced by painters, sculptors, and novelists of the nineteenth century. Emanuel Leutze's *Washington Crossing the Delaware* (Fig. 462), painted in 1851, is a notable example of such romantic imagery. Although it is false in almost every historical detail, this huge canvas has become

458

Fig. 458. Stage Fort Across Gloucester Harbor,
*by Fitz Hugh Lane (1804–65), 1862; oil on
canvas, 38 by 60 inches (95.5 by 152.4 cm.).
Like Heade, Lane concentrated on the effects of
light and atmosphere, most especially as they
manifested themselves in the vicinity of water.
Here Lane paints Gloucester Harbor bathed in
pastel light. The hush that hangs over water and
land alike is almost palpable; nothing moves or
distracts us from the absolute stillness of the scene
and the luminosity of the atmosphere.*
Purchase, Rogers and Fletcher Funds, Erving and
Joyce Wolf Fund, Raymond J. Horowitz Gift, Bequest
of Richard De Wolfe Brixey, by exchange, and John
Osgood and Elizabeth Amis Cameron Blanchard Memorial Fund, 1978 (1978.203)

a widely accepted symbol of Washington's heroic coup on Christmas night of
1776. It is Leutze's most famous picture,
so laden with patriotic sentiment that it
is idle to attempt any aesthetic criticism—except to recall that it is highly
representative of a school of romantic
painting that flourished during the
middle years of the last century at Düsseldorf, Germany, where Leutze was
working at the time he composed this
extraordinary fantasy. In 1851 the president of the American Art-Union claimed that it was "one of the greatest productions of the age, and eminently worthy to commemorate the greatest event
in the military life of the illustrious man
whom all nations delight to honor."

In spite of Leutze's otherwise imaginative rendering of the event, it was in
at least one respect faithful to the facts.
He had taken pains to procure from the
Patent Office in Washington a perfect
copy of the general's clothes. However,
he could not find a German model large
enough to fill them. By the best of fortune the American artist Worthington
Whittredge unexpectedly appeared on
the scene. He was of the required stat-
ure, and Leutze immediately pressed
him into service to pose as the general.
"Spy glass in hand and the other on my

knee," Whittredge recalled, "I stood
and was nearly dead when the operation was over. They poured champagne
down my throat and I lived through it."
He also posed, sitting down, for the
steersman.

In his dynamic depictions of the rugged western mountains, which he made
familiar to most Americans for the first
time, Albert Bierstadt strove for spectacular effects. Such grandiose panoramas as *The Rocky Mountains* (Fig. 464),
freely worked up in his New York studio
from studies made in the field, brought
Bierstadt higher prices than any other
American artist had yet received for his
work. When it was first shown in New
York, this more or less synthetic creation received a tumultuous public welcome.

With such huge, impressive visions of
the western scene it might be said that
the discovery of America by its artists
was almost complete. To satisfy his wish
to record more remote and exotic natural spectacles, Frederic Edwin Church,
a pupil of Thomas Cole, journeyed to
many parts of the world. In South
America he sketched volcanic mountains and such panoramic views as *Heart
of the Andes* (Fig. 463; this painting and
Bierstadt's *Rocky Mountains* are hung to-

459

460

gether, as they were at the New York Sanitary Fair of 1864). Church also traveled to the Arctic, with its frozen wastes and mountains of ice, and to distant Greece, where he sketched the Parthenon, among other subjects. All of this he worked into finished canvases upon returning to his studio. Now, however, the almost photographic detail of these immense compositions, so dear to the Hudson River school, begins to seem a little too insistent.

Fig. 461. Winter in the Country. A Cold Morning, *by Currier and Ives after George H. Durrie, 1864; hand-colored lithograph, 18⁹/₁₆ by 27 inches (47.5 by 68.6 cm.). When most people think of Currier and Ives they think of engaging and homey prints like this, showing lovely rural scenery populated by cheerful folks engaged in such traditional tasks as splitting and stacking wood. Currier and Ives prided themselves on providing prints on such a wide range of subjects that no one could fail to find one—or many more than one—of interest. They described themselves as publishers of "Colored Engravings for the People," and according to their biographer Harry T. Peters, "In their heyday Currier prints were to be found adorning the walls of barrooms, barbershops, firehouses, and hotels, as well as of the homes of rich and poor alike."*
Bequest of Adele S. Colgate, 1962 (63.550.502)

461

462

Fig. 462. Washington Crossing the Delaware, *by Emanuel Leutze (1816–68), 1851; oil on canvas, 149 by 255 inches (378.5 by 647.7 cm.). Leutze, born in Germany and brought to America as a baby, returned to Düsseldorf to study painting in 1841. Düsseldorf was very popular with art students in those days, for its stress on correct drawing and melodramatic historical subjects appealed to would-be artists all over Europe and America. Leutze chose as the subject for this painting the night in December 1776 when General George Washington and a ragged band of troops crossed the Delaware River bound for*

Trenton, New Jersey. Arriving early the next morning, they surprised the Hessian troops, won the ensuing battle, and thus turned the tide of the war.

Numerous errors in historical details have been identified in this painting, and the heroic poses of General Washington and other central figures undoubtedly serve the purposes of artistic composition with more fidelity than those of historical accuracy. Nevertheless, this is a picture that, because it has been reproduced more often than almost any other American painting, has shaped more Americans' concept of the Revolutionary

War than any other. Its importance is in capturing something of the commitment and determination that characterized Washington and other leaders of the period. The drama of this episode, despite the melodrama, rings true.
Gift of John Stewart Kennedy, 1897 (97.34)

482

Fig. 482. **Cremorne Gardens, No. 2,** *by James McNeill Whistler (1834–1903), about 1875; oil on canvas, 27 by 58⅛ inches (68.6 by 134.9 cm.). Whistler's interest in paintings as exercises in formal harmonies led him to do a series of night pieces, which he called nocturnes. The pleasure gardens that give this painting its name flourished briefly in the mid-nineteenth century in the Chelsea section of London where Whistler lived. Fashionably dressed guests stroll about, exchange a word or two, and gather at a table to enjoy refreshments in a painting that captures the essence of a summer night. Light pierces the darkness or highlights a figure, but much of the garden and most of its inhabitants remain lost in the darkness.*
John Stewart Kennedy Fund, 1912 (12.32)

483

484

Fig. 483. **Arrangement in Flesh Colour and Black: Portrait of Théodore Duret,** *by James McNeill Whistler (1834–1903), about 1883; oil on canvas, 76⅛ by 35¾ inches (193.4 by 90.8 cm.). Unlike Eakins, whose portrait of Louis N. Kenton this resembles superficially, Whistler's foremost concern was not portraiture. He was more interested in pure composition, its tensions and its harmonies. Here Duret's boldly painted black suit and snowy shirt and tie stand out sharply against the background, exemplifying American art historian Edgar P. Richardson's description of Whistler's portraits as having broad areas of color "(whose mere breadth was shocking then), without reflections from one to the other, but with long, clean edges, presenting bold contrasts of warm against cool, light against dark, hue against hue."*
Wolfe Fund, Catharine Lorillard Wolfe Collection, 1913 (13.20)

Fig. 484. **Nocturne,** *by James McNeill Whistler (1834–1903), 1878 (printed in 1887); lithotint, 6¾ by 10¼ inches (17.2 by 26 cm.). Whistler was one of the most important printmakers of the nineteenth century; his etchings and lithographs, produced from the late 1850s onward, influenced his contemporaries to revive those arts. Here Whistler uses a grainy texture to convey the quality of the night light—dark and light mixed together to create a dusk-verging-on-dark atmosphere. The river and the land merge, one or two lights twinkle, and the whole composition, as the title suggests, evokes a dreamy, pensive piece for the piano.*
Harris Brisbane Dick Fund, 1917 (17.3.159)

Fig. 485. Madame X (Madame Pierre Gautreau), by John Singer Sargent (1856–1925), 1884; oil on canvas, 82⅛ by 43¼ inches (208.6 by 109.9 cm.). Sargent was born in Florence and studied art in Italy and Paris, but, despite foreign training, he brought to his work an American freshness and willingness to flout tradition. Early in his career he lived in Paris, where he painted Madame Gautreau, an American married to a Paris banker. The finished portrait was exhibited at the Paris Salon of 1884, where it precipitated an uproar. The stark simplicity startled a public not yet exposed to "less is more" aesthetics, and Madame Gautreau's daring décolletage provided a further shock. The subject's mother asked Sargent to remove the painting from exhibition, but he refused. What seemed barbarous to a genteel public seemed fine and bold to hardier viewers, however. In 1887 Henry James wrote of the portrait: "It is full of audacity of experiment and science of execution; it has singular beauty of line, and certainly in the body and arms we feel the pulse of life as strongly as the brush can give it."

Arthur Hoppock Hearn Fund, 1916 (16.53)

Fig. 486. Mr. and Mrs. I. N. Phelps Stokes, by John Singer Sargent (1856–1925), 1897; oil on canvas, 84¼ by 39¾ inches (214 by 101 cm.). Sargent painted this handsome New York couple in London. The portrait was originally to be only of Mrs. Stokes, and many years later Stokes wrote of the occasion that settled her dress and pose in Sargent's mind: "Edith had on a starched white piqué skirt, and a light shirt-waist under her blue serge, tailor-made, jacket. As she came into the studio, full of energy, and her cheeks aglow from the brisk walk, Sargent exclaimed at once: 'I want to paint you just as you are.'" Later it was decided to add Mr. Stokes to the portrait, and although his wife remains the central figure, he is very much a presence in the composition, his tall form echoing and emphasizing hers. The elongation of figures, which makes them so striking, and the emphasis on Mrs. Stokes's costume, with its sharp contrast between white skirt and dark jacket, were criticized when the portrait was exhibited in America. More em-

485

486

phasis should have been given to characterization than to externals, the critics said. Despite these objections, the portrait is both striking and perfectly representative of Sargent's 1890s style in brushwork, composition, and elegant atmosphere. Bequest of Edith Minturn Phelps Stokes (Mrs. I. N.), 1938 (38.104)

Fig. 487. **The Escutcheon of Charles v of Spain,** *by John Singer Sargent (1856–1925), about 1912; watercolor and pencil, 11⅞ by 17¾ inches (30.2 by 45.1 cm.). The intense light of a summer day is seen here shimmering on a carved stone escutcheon; the strong molded arch that encloses the carving provides structure in a composition that might otherwise be difficult to read. The impressionistic works on this page contrast strongly with the more substantial images of Madame Gautreau and Mrs. Stokes on the opposite page.* Purchase, Joseph Pulitzer Bequest, 1915 (15.142.11)

Fig. 488. **Two Girls with Parasols at Fladbury,** *by John Singer Sargent (1856–1925), 1889; oil on canvas, 29½ by 25 inches (74.9 by 63.5 cm.). Although Sargent was much sought-after as a painter of formal portraits, he was happier doing impressionistic landscape studies and sketches. This vivid outdoor scene reveals Monet's influence in both subject matter and brushwork, for here Sargent, as if in revolt from the demands of portraiture, concentrates on color and light, leaving the girls' faces featureless. In fact, by 1909 his discontent had increased to the point where he all but gave up painting portraits to concentrate on capturing the vibrant outdoor light in watercolors.* Gift of Mrs. Francis Ormond, 1950 (50.130.13)

of superb etchings and lithographs he produced throughout his career (Fig. 484). Whistler had many followers, and the influence of his aesthetic theories was considerable.

Whistler was but one of a number of exceptional American artists who preferred to live abroad during their professional careers. His younger contemporary John Singer Sargent, a complete cosmopolitan, chose to remain in London after studying and working in Paris for a period of years. His success as a fashionable portraitist was extraordinary; to be "done" by Sargent at $5,000 and up was considered a distinction and a privilege, well worth the very high fee. His portrait of Madame Pierre Gautreau, entitled *Madame X* (Fig. 485), is a striking characterization of a celebrated beauty and a masterpiece of economical expression. When Sargent offered to sell the canvas to the Museum, he wrote, "I suppose it is the best thing I have done." The Museum has acquired more than a dozen other examples of this artist's work, some of which, such as *Mr. and Mrs. I. N. Phelps Stokes* (Fig. 486), show Sargent's talent for psychological penetration of his subjects. Although it resulted in an admirably fresh and vivid portrait, Sargent labored long and hard on the Stokes painting. He redid the head of Mrs. Stokes nine times before he was satisfied with it.

Later in life he found welcome relief from fashionable portraiture in landscapes such as *Two Girls with Parasols at Fladbury* (Fig. 488), and in watercolors of dazzling charm (Fig. 487). The latter are represented in the Museum's collection by numerous examples. It is no heresy to prefer these private exercises of Sargent's to his commissioned por-

487

488

489

490

Fig. 489. Lydia Crocheting in the Garden at Marly, *by Mary Cassatt (1844–1926), 1880; oil on canvas, 32 by 42 inches (81.3 by 106.7 cm.). Many of Cassatt's paintings are of women—or of mothers and children—and frequently her model was her beloved sister Lydia, as is the case here. The vibrancy of the colors of the garden and the brilliance of Lydia's bonnet emphasize her pallor, which foreshadows her death two years later. A good deal of Cassatt's importance lies in the influence she had on her wealthy art-oriented countrymen, for she imparted her enthusiasm for French impressionist paintings to them and was therefore responsible for some wonderful canvases finding a home in America at an early date. The Havemeyer collection, now at the Metropolitan Museum, is a major example.* Gift of Mrs. Gardner Cassatt, 1965 (65.184)

Fig. 490. Lady at the Tea Table, *by Mary Cassatt (1844–1926), 1885; oil on canvas, 29 by 24 inches (73.7 by 61 cm.). Mary Cassatt was brought up in Pennsylvania and studied at the Pennsylvania Academy of the Fine Arts, but from young womanhood onward she preferred to live in Europe. She established a studio in Paris, became friends with Degas and other members of the still very new impressionist group, and gradually created a style of her own. She and Berthe Morisot were the only women asked to exhibit with the impressionists, and from the 1870s Cassatt showed with them rather than with the more traditional artists at the Paris Salon. In this portrait she places Philadelphia aristocrat Mrs. Robert Moore Riddle in an ambiguous setting—foreground and background are the same color, revealing her debt to Degas, Manet, and Japanese prints, and the bold color scheme emphasizes and repeats the blue and white of the Chinese porcelain tea set. Whistler was among the first to collect this oriental ware as just one aspect of his great appreciation of Eastern art.* Gift of Mary Cassatt, 1923 (23.101)

491

Fig. 491. Woman Bathing, *by Mary Cassatt (1844–1926), 1891; drypoint, soft-ground etching, and aquatint, 14⁵/₁₆ by 10⁹/₁₆ inches (36.5 by 26.8 cm.). In 1890 Cassatt attended an exhibition of Japanese wood-block prints at the Ecole des Beaux-Arts in Paris with her friends Manet and Degas. Like them, she was enormously impressed with the prints, and, besides acquiring some for her own collection, she set about incorporating such elements as their two dimensionality, coloring, and asymmetry into her own work. After much careful experimentation Cassatt produced a series of color prints, of which this is one, that demonstrate her success in closely duplicating the effects of Japanese printmaking.*
Gift of Paul J. Sachs, 1916 (16.2.2)

492

Fig. 492. Ernesta with Nurse, *by Cecilia Beaux (1855–1942), 1894; oil on canvas, 49 by 37 inches (124.5 by 94 cm.). Cecilia Beaux was from a genteel Philadelphia family. Her best work was done around the turn of the century, and here she combines interests in abstract pattern and portraiture to create an unusual and arresting canvas. It is possibly her best-known painting, and one that has always been very popular with viewers. By the end of her long life, Beaux had achieved many honors, though she never became a trend setter.*
Maria DeWitt Jesup Fund, 1965 (65.49)

traits. Painting for himself for a change, unhampered by the need to satisfy a client, and working in a medium natural to his quick and fluid style of recording impressions, his responses were so personal and immediate that it is impossible to remain indifferent to them.

Although Sargent spent most of his life abroad, like Whistler he always considered himself an American at heart and in fact. He refused a British knighthood rather than give up his United States citizenship, which he treasured to the end of his days.

Conspicuous among other American artists abroad was Mary Cassatt, a Pennsylvanian with impeccable social credentials. The first really important American woman artist, she remains among the best. She was, as well, the only American artist who became an established member of the impressionist

group in Paris. She worked with Degas and learned from him, Manet, Renoir, and other French impressionists, but she imitated none of them. She was not interested in painting important people and treated her sitters so impersonally that, except for some members of her own family, few are identified. Apparently she never did a commissioned portrait. The subject in *Lydia Crocheting in the Garden at Marly* (Fig. 489) is the artist's sister, Lydia Cassatt, and *Lady at the Tea Table* (Fig. 490) represents Mrs. Robert Moore Riddle. Cassatt never married and had no children, but she created numerous glowing depictions of mothers and their small children.

Mary Cassatt had an important influence on the development of American taste—at least on the taste of wealthy compatriots whom she introduced to the works of many significant European

493

artists of the past and present and whom she advised in their purchases. Like Whistler, Cassatt was deeply impressed by Japanese prints and, again like Whistler, had she never painted a canvas she would be well remembered for her superb prints (Fig. 491). Her respect for Japanese art is especially evident in these, many colored examples of which are in the Museum's collection.

Cecilia Beaux, another woman artist of Cassatt's generation and also a Pennsylvanian, specialized in portraits, which she executed with imagination and verve. The striking painting *Ernesta with Nurse* (Fig. 492), in which a voluminous skirt, sleeve, and hand are all that is visible of the nurse, shows the spirited composition and bold brushwork for which Beaux was noted.

In his book *Crumbling Idols*, published in 1894, Hamlin Garland wrote that the French impressionists had taught him to see colors everywhere. Their work, he explained, conveyed a "momentary concept of the sense of sight; the stayed and reproduced effect of a single section of the world of color upon the eye." He urged his compatriots to look at their own land in this novel and illuminating way. However, the American artist returning from France had to adjust his sights to the different realities of his native scene and atmosphere. The light in this country was different from that in France, and to those grown accustomed to the picturesquely costumed natives and clustered stone dwellings of Normandy and Brittany, America in its progressive commotion seemed to offer only prosaic counterparts.

J. Alden Weir studied art first with his father, who was professor of drawing at West Point, and then in New York and Paris. In 1895, when he and his family

494

Fig. 495. **The White Kimono,** *by Childe Hassam (1859–1935), 1915; etching and drypoint, $7^7/_{16}$ by $10^{13}/_{16}$ inches (18.9 by 27.5 cm.). Turning to printmaking for the first time in 1915 at the age of fifty-six, Hassam became outstanding in that field. In this example, a woman clad in a kimono stands lost in contemplation before a fireplace—a subject influenced by Japanese art and the work of Whistler. This was a new departure for Hassam, who until now had been in the habit of portraying city scenes and country landscapes.* Harris Brisbane Dick Fund, 1917 (17.3.494)

495

arrived in Windham, Connecticut, for their annual visit, Weir was at first dismayed to find a new cast-iron construction replacing the old covered wooden bridge that spanned the Shetucket River near his house. Then, in a moment of revelation he saw in that stark red-coated replacement the subject of a luminous painting in a setting of summer verdure. He labeled it quite simply *The Red Bridge* (Fig. 493).

During his sojourn in France, Childe Hassam learned the technique and the palette of the impressionists, to lay on his canvases the brilliant synthetic pigments that were then available in separate, small flecks for the eye of the observer to mix in its own way. This he did in his painting *Spring Morning in the Heart of the City* (Fig. 494), although here as in other examples of his work he did not emphasize color vibrations at the expense of the forms he depicted. As he grew older Hassam's interest in printmaking grew stronger (Fig. 495), finally taking precedence over his painting.

The contingent of American impressionists and post-impressionists included such other disparate and talented artists as Maurice Prendergast, Edmund C. Tarbell, John H. Twachtman, and, among still others represented in the collection, William Merritt Chase. Chase was the most influential of the group, for in his lifetime he probably instructed more art students than any other American, including Benjamin West. Early in his professional career on the Continent he worked very successfully in a broad manner that recalled the slashing brushstrokes of Hals, Rubens, and Velázquez. As he approached middle age back in America, Chase lightened his palette, and in

496

Fig. 496. **Central Park,** *by Maurice Prendergast (1859–1924), 1908–10; oil on canvas, $20^3/_4$ by 27 inches (52.7 by 68.6 cm.). This cheerful, supremely colorful scene in New York's Central Park is the result of years of European travel and study. Early in his career Prendergast worked in watercolor, developing a fresh, personal style. When he turned to painting in oils, he adapted many of his watercolor scenes to the new medium, often reworking them over and over, as he has done here. This scene is thought to date from 1903, but Prendergast's assured handling of the oils would place the date of this particular canvas at about 1908–10. His technique is based on the French post-impressionist one of applying dots and blobs of color, one next to the other, so that the scene seems to shimmer on the canvas. The picture is held in place by the strong horizontal and vertical lines, however, created by the benches and roadway and by the trees that thrust upward across the canvas.* George A. Hearn Fund, 1950 (50.25)

498

scenes such as *At the Seaside* and *For the Little One* (Figs. 498 and 499) he applied brilliant colors with a masterful technique and with enormous zest. Chase experimented with printmaking too, and *Reverie* (Fig. 497) is a monotype that has the richness of a painting.

John H. Twachtman, occasional painting companion and friend of most of the men just mentioned, pictured *Arques-la-Bataille* (Fig. 503), a site near Dieppe on the Normandy coast, in a subtle orchestration of subdued colors. Delicate grays, greens, and blues are thinly and broadly applied in a manner that evokes an image of the landscape rather than defines it and is reminiscent of the tonal harmonies of Whistler.

The post-impressionist style was represented in America by Maurice Prendergast, who had been particularly influenced by the work of Pierre Bonnard and Edouard Vuillard when he studied in France. His work reflects his fascination with brilliant primary colors and surface texture. Art historian Jules Prown's observation that Prendergast's "delight in blobs of color manifested itself in a fascination with balloons, parasols and banners" is borne out by the Museum's *Central Park* (Fig. 496).

John White Alexander, yet another American who studied and lived in Europe, was one of our leading artists at the turn of the century. His *Repose* (Fig. 504), a strikingly elegant recumbent female figure, shows the influence of his friend Whistler in its delicate brushwork and thin paint surfaces as well as of the Art Nouveau movement in its composition.

The present century has witnessed extraordinary changes in the arts as in everything else, and they have been at times both violent and confusing. At the

499

Fig. 498. At the Seaside, *by William Merritt Chase (1844–1916), about 1892; oil on canvas, 20 by 34 inches (50.8 by 86.4 cm.). A native of Indiana, Chase studied there and in New York and St. Louis before being sent to Europe by a group of St. Louis businessmen. (When they inquired whether Chase would like such a trip, he responded "I'd rather go to Europe than go to heaven.") Returning to America in 1878, he took a studio at 51 West Tenth Street in New York and embarked on his successful career as prolific painter and printmaker and extremely influential teacher. For many years he conducted summer art classes at Shinnecock on Long Island, where he had a house and where this impressionist beach scene was painted. The freely disposed brushstrokes and bright, clear colors represent Chase's response to French impressionist painting; it was this response that he passed along to a generation of American artists who studied with him.*
Bequest of Miss Adelaide Milton de Groot (1876–1967), 1967 (67.187.123)

Fig. 499. For the Little One, *by William Merritt Chase (1844–1916), about 1895; oil on canvas, 40 by 35¼ inches (101.6 by 89.5 cm.). As was often his custom in the nineties, Chase here depicts an intimate family picture, showing Mrs. Chase sewing beside a window in their Shinnecock house. Light pours onto the crumpled fabric Mrs. Chase is working and onto the expanse of bare polished floor in the foreground—an unusual innovation. The flood of light from the window creates a diagonal line from the foreground to Mrs. Chase and to the space between the slightly parted curtains. In the center of the window Chase hung a monotype very like the one illustrated in Fig. 497.*
Amelia B. Lazarus Fund, by exchange, 1913 (13.90)

500

Fig. 500. The Masquerade Dress: Portrait of Mrs. Robert Henri, *by Robert Henri (1865–1929), 1911; oil on canvas, 76½ by 36¼ inches (194.2 by 92 cm.). Henri studied art both in Philadelphia and in Paris, becoming a force in the art world first of Philadelphia and later of New York. He had advanced notions about art and artists, believing that work of all kinds should be shown in exhibitions without the formality of jury selection. He was an original member of the group later known as the Ash Can school, whose members believed that beauty is everywhere, even among the ash cans of teeming big-city streets. This portrait of his wife is a more conventional subject, however. Striking in its verticality, emphasized by the stripes of Mrs. Henri's dress, and in its juxtaposition of dark and light, it has, as well, an oriental aspect.* Arthur Hoppock Hearn Fund, 1958 (58.157)

start, new and challenging forces were making themselves felt in American art. In 1908 eight artists showed their work at the Macbeth Gallery in New York; their exhibition was a revolt of sorts. They were all more or less familiar with advanced trends in European painting and with the work of the older Continental masters as well, but while they did not exile themselves in Paris or London, they did take issue with the current artistic trends of the academies. The Eight, as they named themselves and as they will probably always be called— Robert Henri, John Sloan, George Luks, Maurice Prendergast, Ernest Lawson, Everett Shinn, Arthur B. Davies, and William Glackens—were all individuals in their styles and techniques. They were determined that the artist should have freedom and opportunity to express his message in his own way and, for the most part, they saw in the ordinary person and the commonplace scene, even among the ash cans of the teeming cities, a poetry worthy of the artist's brush. It was their choice of subject matter rather than their technical approach that set them apart from the approved academic art of their time. Following Eakins's counsel to artists, they peered deep into the heart of American life to give vital meaning to their work. Several of them had been newspaper and magazine illustrators and were thus practiced in realistic portrayals of daily urban life as they came across it in the course of their reportorial rounds. Collectively they are commonly referred to as the "Ash Can

501

Fig. 501. **Central Park in Winter,** *by William James Glackens (1870–1938), 1905; oil on canvas, 25 by 30 inches (63.5 by 76.2 cm.).* "William Glackens," wrote curator Henry Geldzahler, "produced the most consistently happy paintings of his period." Using approaches borrowed widely from American and French artists he admired, Glackens created this cheery view of activists and onlookers on a snowy day in Central Park. Applying small, feathery strokes in the manner of Renoir, the artist produced in this early period impressionistic scenes that focused on anecdotal details. Glackens was a graphic artist and illustrator whose only formal training took place in night classes. He worked for several newspapers during his career, meeting there such contemporaries as John Sloan, George Luks, and Everett Shinn, all eventual members of the iconoclastic group now known as The Eight.
George A. Hearn Fund, 1921 (21.164)

502

school," but, more accurately, they were New York realists.

Paintings by all eight of these men are represented in the Museum's collection. By no means were all their canvases devoted to street scenes. The catholicity they showed in their choices of subject matter, which drew some censure at the time, is revealed in numerous canvases, for example Henri's broadly painted *The Masquerade Dress* (Fig. 500), a portrait of his wife that reflects his admiration for Hals, Velázquez, and Manet.

Fig. 502. **Unicorns (Legend—Sea Calm),** *by Arthur B. Davies (1862–1928), 1906; oil on canvas, 18¼ by 40¼ inches (46.4 by 102.2 cm.).* Davies studied art in Chicago and New York, and, like a number of other members of The Eight, worked as an illustrator. He is most famous for his early, dreamlike paintings, as seen in his masterpiece, Unicorns. Here the unreal, mythical aspects of Davies's inspiration are emphasized by the unicorns, imaginary creatures attended by equally unworldly maidens. The mountains and smooth, still water heighten the dreamy atmosphere. Davies exhibited with The Eight not because he shared his contemporaries' interest in the hurly-burly of city life, but because he believed in more freedom to exhibit unconventional works. He was a major organizer of the revolutionary Armory Show of 1913, presenting to his stunned countrymen the avant-garde styles of European artists.
Bequest of Lillie P. Bliss, 1931 (31.67.12)

503

504

Fig. 503. Arques-la-Bataille, *by John H. Twachtman (1853–1902), 1885; oil on canvas, 60 by 78⅞ inches (152.4 by 200.3 cm.). Twachtman was born in Cincinnati and began his career painting floral decorations on window shades in his father's business. He soon moved onward and upward, however, studying with Frank Duveneck and accompanying him to Munich to work there. He met, traveled with, and painted with many of the leading American artists of his generation, including Hassam, Robinson, and Chase. He executed this painting, his greatest work, from a sketch he made during an expedition to the Normandy coast. His interest in the landscape is decorative rather than literal: the strong horizontals, succeeding one another in strata of gray and green from the foreground to the background, are counteracted by clumps of reeds that provide strong, dark vertical accents.* Morris K. Jesup Fund, 1968 (68.52)

Central Park in Winter (Fig. 501), painted by Glackens in 1905, tells a happy anecdote of children sleighing. It was quickly apprehended, without resort to unnecessary detail. John Sloan's etching *Turning Out the Light* (Fig. 505) deals with an Ash Can subject—stressing everyday life in all its ordinariness or drabness. Joseph Pennell was a noted illustrator and printmaker who, though not a member of the Ash Can school, shared these urban painters' interest in the world around them—especially in the architecture of cities and factories. In *From Cortlandt Street Ferry* (Fig. 506) he captures the atmosphere of downtown Manhattan at night as it would have appeared to a passenger arriving at the Cortlandt Street slip on the ferry from New Jersey. In an entirely different vein, Arthur B. Davies's *Unicorns* (Fig. 502), probably his most famous work, presents a scene withdrawn from reality into a tranquil, lyrical world of the artist's imagination. The poetic symbolism is too dreamlike for explanation.

At the famous Armory Show of 1913, Arthur B. Davies and Walt Kuhn, with the assistance of other vanguard artists, staged a large exhibition of modern art, both American and foreign. The major impact of that great exhibition came not from the American work but from the international section where, for the first time, Americans at large experienced the shock of fauvism, cubism, expressionism, and other phases of abstract painting and sculpture as those movements had developed in Europe over the preceding twenty or thirty years. From then on, "modern art" became a phrase to conjure with in this country, a battle cry that continues to evoke strong feelings ranging from great enthusiasm to utter revulsion.

Throughout this discussion, we have seen American art develop from a tiny imported seedling into a robust, wide-branching growth of variegated character, constantly invigorated by grafts of alien strains, as it still is, but always sinking its roots deeper into native soil. In later years, American painting and sculpture have spread out in an almost bewildering variety of unprecedented forms. This country, particularly New York City, has become an international capital of art; what is done here is at its best widely accepted as a standard of performance.

Fig. 504. Repose, *by John White Alexander (1856–1915), 1895; oil on canvas, 52¼ by 63⅝ inches (132.7 by 161.6 cm.). This daring portrait is one in a series of figure studies that stress the long, sinuous, sensuous lines of the female figure. But like so much work of this period, the design is the important thing, and the figure simply a means to that end. In emphasizing elongated flowing lines, Alexander was reflecting the influence of the Art Nouveau movement. He lived in Paris during the 1890s and belonged to a circle of prominent artists, poets, and writers that included Whistler, Henry James, and Oscar Wilde.*
Gift of Irina A. Reed, 1980 (1980.224)

Fig. 505. Turning Out the Light, *by John Sloan (1871–1951), 1906; etching, 5 by 7 inches (12.7 by 17.8 cm.). Sloan moved from Philadelphia to New York City in 1904, and applied his considerable talents as an etcher to the city scene. Turning Out the Light is one of his "New York City Life" series, in which ordinary people are seen leading ordinary lives. The commonness of such subjects offended many people who were used to thinking of art as dealing only with conventional subjects, such as landscapes or people carefully posed in their Sunday best. Sloan's dedication to realism lasted throughout his lifetime, though he shifted his interests from time to time in the kind of realism he portrayed. When the Armory Show revealed the state of art in Europe—cubism, abstraction, for example—Sloan's approach seemed conventional by contrast.*
Gift of Gertrude Vanderbilt Whitney, 1926 (26.30.16)

505

506

Fig. 506. From Cortlandt Street Ferry, *by Joseph Pennell (1857–1926), 1908; sandpaper mezzotint, 12¹⁵⁄₁₆ by 9¹³⁄₁₆ inches (32.9 by 24.9 cm.). The artist, who became well known both at home and abroad, was a great friend and admirer of Whistler, and his work was often compared to that of the older artist. Here, in a shadowy night scene reminiscent of Whistler's, Pennell captures the excitement of New York on a rainy night— shimmering light and rain fall between the skyscrapers towering in the foreground, creating a path on the water in front of the oncoming ferry. After the First World War, Pennell settled in New York and established the graphics department at the Art Students League.*
Harris Brisbane Dick Fund, 1917 (17.3.799)

SCULPTURE

The Colonial and Federal Periods 1630–1830

The earliest American sculptors were the skilled woodworkers who in the seventeenth and eighteenth centuries specialized in the ornamental carvings that grace some of the finest examples of furniture in The American Wing collection. Men of similar talents provided figureheads for colonial vessels and occasionally portrait busts and allegorical figures of somewhat primitive character. To these pioneering artists should be added the stonecutters who worked their grim designs on early tombstones.

Fig. 508. **The White Captive,** *by Erastus Dow Palmer (1817–1904), 1859; marble, height 66 inches (167.6 cm.). While many of his countrymen were going abroad to study sculpture, Palmer remained at home working, for the most part, on American subjects. The White Captive was apparently inspired by stories of abductions of white settlers by the Indians. One critic said that it was among the finest sculptures created in America up to that time, and went on, ". . . nothing so fine had come over the seas from Italy; nothing so original, so dramatic, so human; nothing that could approach it even in charm of workmanship."*
Bequest of Hamilton Fish, 1894 (94.93)

508

The Mid-Nineteenth Century, 1840–65

Then, in the second third of the nineteenth century an American school of marble sculpture came into sudden and unexpected bloom. The United States had emerged from the War of 1812—the second war for independence, as it has been called—with a self-consciousness and self-confidence that mounted over time. Those were years of ascendant democracy in this country, leading to the election of Andrew Jackson as president in 1828. Americans were eager to identify their own personal and political virtues with those of the republics of antiquity. Among other things, sympathy for contemporary Greeks who, in the 1820s, were engaged in a war of independence from Turkish domination, added zest to an admiration for ancient Greek models and the Roman copies and adaptations they inspired.

It was in Italy that ancient sculptures and copies of them could be seen and studied with profit, and these strongly influenced the first American sculptors who went there to practice their art. Most of these "Yankee stonecutters" went to Italy for experience and guidance, and a number of them remained. There good marble was abundant and wages of expert stonecutters were low. The aspiring sculptor could give a plaster model to a local craftsman and depend upon him to chisel a faithful replica in enduring marble, an operation often not within the capacity of the original artist. It was just one further advantage that in Italy artists could model nudes without suffering the social criticism that greeted such exposures in America—at least unless they were presented in the guise of figures of some acceptable allegorical significance rather than simply as attractive naked fe-

males. As late as the 1860s one French visitor to the United States observed that, generally speaking, the depiction of a woman's natural form was "not permitted . . . beyond the head and the extremities."

A graceful life-size marble nude with decidedly allegorical trappings is *The White Captive* (Fig. 508), fashioned by Erastus Dow Palmer in the neoclassical style—a mode remarkably popular throughout the Western world in the middle years of the last century. Palmer, a self-taught New Yorker, never went abroad for study. He worked from living models, often one of his daughters, and although this was his first attempt at such a subject, *The White Captive* remains one of the finest of its kind made in America in the last century. It seems to have been inspired by tales of the Indians' captives along the colonial frontier, and it quickly won nationwide attention.

When Vermont-born Hiram Powers left for Italy in 1837, John Quincy Adams composed a bit of doggerel urging the artist to:

Go forth, and rival Greece's art sublime;
Return, and bid the statesmen of thy land
Live in thy marble through all after-time!

Powers never did return to America; he spent most of his professional career in Florence, where he acquired an international reputation. His bust of *President Andrew Jackson* (Fig. 509) is a characteristic and outstanding instance of the American approach to portraiture—a solidly realistic likeness in a neoclassic manner. In 1835 Powers modeled the grizzled, toothless, sixty-eight-year-old war veteran and president to the life, as Jackson had requested. And in 1837 he cut the marble version in Italy.

509

Fig. 509. **President Andrew Jackson,** *by Hiram Powers (1805–73), 1837; marble, height 34½ inches (87.6 cm). Powers considered this moving portrait of Andrew Jackson to be one of his finest works. He was at first reluctant to show the president as he looked at age sixty-eight, but Jackson admonished him, "Make me as I am, Mr. Powers, and be true to nature always. . . . I have no desire to look young as long as I feel old. . . ." Powers carved Jackson's bust in marble himself instead of handing the plaster model over to an Italian stonecutter, as was customary in those days.*
Gift of Mrs. Frances V. Nash, 1894 (94.14)

Fig. 512. Cleopatra, *by William Wetmore Story (1819–95), 1858, this version 1869; marble, height 54½ inches (138.4 cm.).* The public that received this statue of Cleopatra with such enthusiasm was interested at least as much in historical and story-telling aspects of works of art as they were in artistic technique and insight. Here Story presents Cleopatra brooding on her life as she faces her death. The glamour of this beautiful and powerful queen's life—the intrigues and stormy affairs—was fascinating to romantically minded Victorians. But didacticism was equally important, and the fact that Cleopatra's recklessly romantic way of life led to her downfall is an important part of the message here.
Gift of John Taylor Johnson, 1888 (88.5)

510

511

Powers's contemporaries ranked him with the greatest sculptors of antiquity and the Renaissance—a judgment that today seems more than extravagant, simply absurd. However that may be, it reminds us that we all too often tend to use the present as an absolute standard for judging the past—a tendency that reduces much that qualified contemporaries once deemed important to the level of seeming merely quaint. This is also absurd for, properly understood, no achievement of the past remains merely quaint. As we are frequently reminded, viewing the past perceptively and for its own sake may lead to better ways of evaluating the present. We can thus, at least, hope to escape from what the late Bertrand Russell referred to as "the parochialism of time." It is one of the large purposes of the Museum, with its enormously varied collections, to provide this escape.

It might be noted in passing that Powers was something more than an artist. To the end of his days he remained as well an "ingenious Yankee mechanic"—an inventor of tools, instruments, and machines that worked well. He was also a strangely farsighted visionary who discussed with his friend Nathaniel Hawthorne the practicalities of an improved plan for laying transatlantic cables, and who prophesied the feasibility of flying machines and the possibility of life on distant planets. Beyond that, he was handsome and a superb conversationalist. Such an uncommon combination of attributes won him the close and cherished friendship of, among others, Robert and Elizabeth Barrett Browning, who knew him in Florence. (Mrs. Browning once observed that his eyes were so commanding that she won-

Fig. 510. Andrew Jackson, *by William H. Rumney (1837–1927), about 1860; pine, painted, height 78¼ inches (198.8 cm.).* This life-size portrait of the seventh president shows him at his most commanding and dignified, and makes a fine contrast to Powers's portrait. The sculptor was a ship's-figurehead carver, and his work is bold and direct, as a figurehead has to be. Ordered by a prominent shipwright to stand before his East Boston home, the figure is painted white to simulate marble. The pose is taken from a painting of Jackson by Ralph E. W. Earl.
Purchase, Rogers Fund, The J. M. Kaplan Fund, Inc. and Mrs. Frederick A. Stoughton Gifts, Harris Brisbane Dick and Louis V. Bell Funds, 1978 (1978.57)

Fig. 511. Eagle, *attributed to Wilhelm Schimmel (1817–90), nineteenth century; wood, painted, height 12 inches (30.5 cm.).* Schimmel's life was as colorful as his carvings. Though details remain sketchy, he is believed to have wandered about the countryside in Cumberland County, Pennsylvania, paying for his food and drink with his carvings. His eagles, produced with a jackknife, smoothed with bits of broken glass, and painted with whatever colors Schimmel could obtain, have a rugged and vigorous liveliness that is lacking in many other wooden toys.
Gift of Mrs. Robert W. de Forest, 1934 (34.100.169)

Fig. 513. The Babes in the Wood, *by Thomas Crawford (about 1813–57), 1851; marble, length 48½ inches (123.2 cm.). Crawford shows here two children lost in the woods who die in one another's arms. The subject was popular with both the public and other artists of the time, and Crawford's inspiration was very likely an engraving that appeared in the* London Art Journal *in 1847. The sculptor also created many larger works, including the* Armed Liberty *or* Freedom *atop the Capitol in Washington.*
Bequest of Hamilton Fish, 1894 (94.9.4)

Fig. 514. Latona and Her Children Apollo and Diana, *by William Henry Rinehart (1825–74), 1875; marble, height 46 inches (116.8 cm.). Like Story, Rinehart went to Italy to study sculpture, and was so smitten that he decided to take up permanent residence there. Here he portrays Latona, goddess of night, with her children by Jupiter. The characters are of course drawn from classical mythology and the poses and figures are idealized, but Rinehart has begun to exhibit, too, an interest in the realism that characterized the succeeding generation of sculptors.*
Rogers Fund, 1905 (05.12)

513

514

dered "if they claved the marble without the help of his hands.")

While most American sculptors were flocking to Italy to have their works chiseled in marble, stay-at-home craftsmen were turning out an abundance of figures carved in wood. Their free-standing portraits are far less numerous than likenesses painted on canvas or paper, but they include examples that are vigorous statements of personality. These efforts have been referred to as "country whittling developed to a fine art." Thus the rugged, almost forbidding presence of Andrew Jackson is strongly expressed in the full-length portrait of the warrior-president carved by one William Rumney (Fig. 510). An interesting comparison can be made between this figure and Hiram Powers's marble bust of Jackson. Another, much more primitive but equally effective, wooden figure is that of a painted eagle by Wilhelm Schimmel. For some years after the Civil War, this itinerant German immigrant whittled toys and mantel ornaments for the inhabitants of snug Cumberland County, Pennsylvania, farmhouses. The businesslike eagle seen here (Fig. 511) is typical of Schimmel's many carvings of the national bird.

Thomas Crawford and William Wetmore Story, both of good family and with influential social and political associations, turned to the practice of sculpture as young men. Working largely in Rome, they earned enviable reputations in the years immediately preceding the Civil War. A typical nineteenth-century romantic, Story infused his subjects with literary allusions. He was a friend of Nathaniel Hawthorne, who described him as a "perplexing variety of talents and accomplishments— . . . being a

apply principles of light and color . . . to indicate very carefully in every part, the exact time of day and circumstance of light." Today he is best remembered as the first American master of the fusion of decorative art and architecture. Before Tiffany, he worked with stained glass as no American had before him. His "Welcome" window (see Fig. 409), completed in 1909 and now on display in the southwest corner of the courtyard, has been termed one of the crowning achievements of his career. In it, his passionate interest in light and color came into full play.

The only contemporary sculptor to approach Saint-Gaudens's fame was Daniel Chester French, who had once studied anatomy with Rimmer. His approach to art was relatively conservative and upheld the academic tradition of his time with elegant style. French's Melvin Memorial, commonly known as *Mourning Victory* (Fig. 519), is a marble copy of a monument he created in 1909 as a memorial to three brothers of the Melvin family who had died in the Civil War and who were buried in Sleepy Hollow Cemetery, Concord, Massachusetts, where French's original marks their graves.

French enjoyed a long and illustrious professional career: in 1873, when he was in his early twenties and far from proven as an artist, he was commissioned to execute the bronze statue of the minuteman that still stands in Concord. It won him immediate fame, and forty-eight long years later he created the statue of Abraham Lincoln for the famous memorial to that president at Washington.

In the final decades of the last century the American West was completing an epic cycle. The frontier, so long a significant feature of American experience, was officially declared closed in 1890. With some good reason Frederic Sackrider Remington considered himself *the* artist-reporter of the rapidly vanishing ways of life along these vast borderlands where army troopers, cowboys, and Indians acted out the finale of an almost legendary drama. His action-charged paintings remain a vivid guide for those who try to visualize the passing of the Wild West. Theodore Roosevelt predicted that the cowboys would live for all time in the bronze figures of Remington, such as *The Mountain Man* (Fig. 520).

Struggle of the Two Natures in Man (see Fig. 7), a freestanding group cut in marble by George Grey Barnard, depicts the divine nature of man casting off his earthly self and reaching for the heavens. Like Saint-Gaudens, Barnard studied at the Ecole des Beaux-Arts, and like Saint-Gaudens he worked in a naturalistic vein. However, his typical subjects show no influence from academic French styles. Rather, they express a passionate romanticism and a rebellious disregard for the canons of art observed by his conservative contemporaries. His *Two Natures* is a dramatic work, with figures considerably larger than life-size. It clearly reveals his admiration for the sculptures of Michelangelo and of Auguste Rodin, Barnard's somewhat older French contemporary and another highly independent spirit. Barnard was a poor and lonely young student in Paris when he modeled this monumental composition in 1891. When the marble version (which he cut himself) was first shown to the public in 1894, it was highly praised by French critics. Predictably, Rodin was among the many who admired the work

521

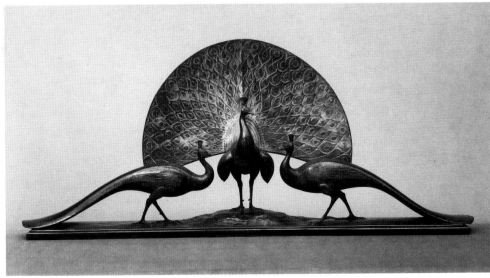

522

Fig. 523. **Figure of Dignity—Irish Mountain Goat,** *by John Bernard Flannagan (1895–1942), granite and aluminum, about 1932; height 53¾ inches with base (136.5 cm.). Largely self-taught, Flannagan progressed from wood to stone carving. He liked to work in the country, selecting stones from the fields and letting their shapes suggest his sculptures. In Mountain Goat, the animal and the stone are literally fused, each giving meaning to the other. The rough texture of the granite emphasizes the nature of both the stone and of the hardy mountain goat that arises from it. The cast-aluminum horns that contribute markedly to the effectiveness of the sculpture are a witty touch.*
Gift of The Alexander Shilling Fund, 1941 (41.47)

Fig. 524. **Mother and Child,** *by William Zorach (1889–1966), about 1930; marble, height 65 inches (165.1 cm.). Although he exhibited Fauvist paintings at the 1913 Armory Show, by the 1920s Zorach had decided to concentrate on sculpture. He was among the first (along with Flannagan) to revive the direct-carving method of sculpture, in which the artist works directly on the stone from start to finish with no intermediate models. Here the intertwined figures of mother and child provide an intricate interplay of line and mass. As John Baur wrote in the catalogue to an exhibition of Zorach's works at the Whitney Museum, "the flowing progression of the main forms and of the spaces between them, the relaxed turn of heads and bodies all lead the eye around*

the piece, up and down, forward and backward with a slow and fugue-like rhythm."
Fletcher Fund, 1952 (52.143)

523

and were impressed by its expressive powers. Barnard was just thirty-one years old at the time. In later years he formed a collection of medieval French stonework that became the nucleus of The Cloisters, the Metropolitan Museum's collection of medieval art at Fort Tryon Park in New York City.

As the present century advanced, the quite literal naturalism of the sculptors just mentioned gave way to a simplification of form that is compellingly illustrated by Paul Manship's highly stylized bronze composition, *Dancer and Gazelles* (Fig. 521). When he won the Prix de Rome in 1909—he was twenty-four years old at the time—Paul Manship went to the Academy in Rome for further study, bypassing Paris and the Ecole des Beaux-Arts. There he became fascinated by the examples of archaic Greek art and other works of classical antiquity that he saw in and about that timeless city. The experience strongly influenced Manship's subsequent development as an artist and can be discerned in the graceful curving rhythms, the fastidiously executed drapery folds, and the finely articulated anatomical details of the *Dancer*. However, although Manship used classical subjects for many of his sculptures, his renderings of these were his own and were explicitly modern in spirit. Upon his return to America, Manship enjoyed a great vogue through such works as this one, another entitled *Centaur and Dryad*, and others owned by the Museum. One eminent critic referred to him as "the most hopeful figure in native sculpture." All New Yorkers and visitors to the metropolis are familiar with Manship's prominently displayed *Prometheus*, the soaring gilded bronze figure in the sunken plaza of Rockefeller Center.

In his bronze *The Peacocks* (Fig. 522), the French émigré sculptor Gaston Lachaise, a sometime assistant to Manship, shows a debt to the latter's style in the bold emphasis on linear pattern. (Lachaise worked with Manship on the completion of the stone tablet in memory of John Pierpont Morgan installed in the Great Hall of the Museum.) He soon abandoned such decorative and ornamental mannerisms in favor of forms of voluptuous roundness, and it was with these that he earned a reputation that ranked him among the greatest sculptors of the period. John B. Flannagan's *Irish Mountain Goat* (Fig. 523) rises directly from the rough piece of fieldstone that both serves as the goat's base and is part of its body—a reference to the oneness of things that Flannagan stressed over and over in his work. Both the streamlined form of the goat and the deliberate choice of ordinary yellowish stone instead of the smooth marble or metal favored by Beaux-Arts sculptors mark Flannagan as a modernist.

Mother and Child (Fig. 524) was chiseled directly in marble by the Lithuanian-born William Zorach between 1927 and 1930. The freshly aroused interest in direct stone-carving seen in both Flannagan's and Zorach's work brought with it a new emphasis on form and solidity that shows the influence of cubism, a style with which Zorach had become familiar when he first visited France in 1910. However, the relatively abstract quality of the resulting design does not reduce the living expressiveness of the figures here. In the decade following the completion of this work, Zorach became a leader of the modern movement in this country.

Selected Bibliography

Besides the following works and consultations with the curators, clippings and unpublished reports in the American Wing files provided material for captions.

General

Brooklyn Museum. *The American Renaissance, 1875–1917*. New York: Pantheon Books, 1979.

Butler, Joseph T. *American Antiques, 1800–1900*. New York: Odyssey Press, 1965.

Clark, Robert Judson, ed. *The Arts and Crafts Movement in America 1876–1916*. Princeton: Princeton University Press, 1972.

Comstock, Helen, ed. *The Concise Encyclopedia of American Antiques*. 2 vols. New York: Hawthorne Books, n.d.

Cooper, Wendy A. *In Praise of America, American Decorative Arts, 1650–1830 / Fifty Years of Discovery Since the 1929 Girl Scouts Loan Exhibition*. New York: Alfred A. Knopf, 1980.

Davidson, Marshall B., author and editor in charge. *The American Heritage History of Colonial Antiques*. New York: American Heritage Publishing Co., 1967.

———. *The American Heritage History of American Antiques from the Revolution to the Civil War*. New York: American Heritage Publishing Co., 1968.

———. *The American Heritage History of Antiques from the Civil War to World War I*. New York: American Heritage Publishing Co., 1969.

Earle, Alice Morse. *Customs and Fashions in Old New England*. Reprint. Rutland, Vt.: Charles E. Tuttle Co., 1975.

Howe, Katherine S., and Warren, David B. *The Gothic Revival Style in America, 1830–1870*. Houston: Museum of Fine Arts, 1976.

Mayhew, Edgar deN., and Myers, Minor, Jr. *A Documentary History of American Interiors from the Colonial Era to 1915*. New York: Charles Scribner's Sons, 1980.

Sprigg, June. *By Shaker Hands*. New York: Alfred A. Knopf, 1975.

Stillinger, Elizabeth. *The ANTIQUES Guide to Decorative Arts in America, 1600–1875*. New York: E. P. Dutton and Co., 1972.

Tracy, Berry B., and Gerdts, William H. *Classical America, 1815–1845*. Newark, N.J.: The Newark Museum, 1963.

Tracy, Berry B., Johnson, Marilynn, and others. *19th-Century America, Furniture and Other Decorative Arts*. New York: The Metropolitan Museum of Art, 1970.

Period Rooms and Furniture

Andrews, Edward Deming, and Andrews, Faith. *Shaker Furniture*. New York: Dover Publications, Inc., 1950.

Art and Antiques, ed. *Nineteenth Century Furniture, Innovation, Revival and Reform*. New York: Art and Antiques, 1982.

Baillie, G. H., Clutton, C., and Ilbert, C. A. *Britten's Old Clocks and Watches and Their Makers*. Reprint. New York: Bonanza Books, 1955.

Baltimore Museum of Art. *Baltimore Furniture, The Work of Baltimore Cabinetworkers from 1760 to 1810*. Baltimore, 1947.

———. *Baltimore Painted Furniture 1800–1840*. Baltimore, 1972.

Battison, Edwin A., and Kane, Patricia E. *The American Clock 1725–1865*. Greenwich, Conn.: New York Graphic Society Limited, 1973.

Bishop, Robert. *The American Chair, Three Centuries of Style*. Reprint. New York: Bonanza Books, 1983.

Bishop, Robert, and Coblentz, Patricia. *The World of Antiques, Art, and Architecture in Victorian America*. New York: E. P. Dutton, 1979.

Bjerkoe, Ethel Hall. *The Cabinetmakers of America*. New York: Bonanza Books, 1957.

Blake, Peter. *Frank Lloyd Wright, Architecture and Space*. Baltimore: Penguin Books, 1965.

Bordes, Marilynn Johnson. *Baltimore Federal Furniture*. New York: The Metropolitan Museum of Art, 1972.

Colonial Society of Massachusetts. *Boston Furniture of the Eighteenth Century*. Boston, 1974. Distributor: The University Press of Virginia.

Comstock, Helen. *American Furniture, Seventeenth, Eighteenth, and Nineteenth Century Styles*. New York: The Viking Press, 1962.

Currier Gallery of Art. *The Dunlaps & Their Furniture*. Manchester, N.H., 1970.

Fairbanks, Jonathan L., and Bates, Elizabeth Bidwell. *American Furniture 1620 to the Present*. New York: Richard Marek Publishers, 1981.

Fairbanks, Jonathan L., and Trent, Robert F. *New England Begins: The Seventeenth Century*. 3 vols. Boston: Museum of Fine Arts, 1982.

Fales, Dean A., Jr. *American Painted Furniture 1660–1880*. New York: E. P. Dutton, 1972.

Gruber, Francis. *The Art of Joinery, 17th-Century Case Furniture in The American Wing*. New York: The Metropolitan Museum of Art, 1972.

Hanks, David A. *The Decorative Designs of Frank Lloyd Wright*. New York: E. P. Dutton, 1979.

———. *Innovative Furniture in America from 1800 to the Present*. New York: Horizon Press, 1981.

Heckscher, Morrison H. "Form and Frame: New Thoughts on the American Easy Chair," *The Magazine Antiques*, Dec. 1971, pp. 886–93.

———. "John Townsend's Block-and-Shell Furniture," *The Magazine Antiques*, May 1982, pp. 1144–52.

———. "The New York Serpentine Card Table," *The Magazine Antiques*, May 1973, pp. 974–83.

Hornor, William Macpherson, Jr. *Blue Book, Philadelphia Furniture, William Penn to George Washington*. Reprint. Washington, D.C.: Highland House Publishers, 1977.

Johnston, William R. "Anatomy of the Chair: American Regional Variations in Eighteenth Century Styles," *The Metropolitan Museum of Art Bulletin* n.s. xxi (Nov. 1962), pp. 118–29.

Kane, Patricia E. *300 Years of American Seating Furniture, Chairs and Beds from the Mabel Brady Garvan and Other Collections at Yale University*. Boston: New York Graphic Society, 1976.

Kaufmann, Edgar, Jr. "Frank Lloyd Wright at The Metropolitan Museum of Art," *The Metropolitan Museum of Art Bulletin* XL, no. 2 (Fall 1982).

Landreau, Anthony N. *America Underfoot, A History of Floor Coverings from Colonial Times to the Present*. Washington, D.C.: Smithsonian Institution Press, 1976.

Loth, Calder, and Sadler, Julius Trousdale, Jr. *The Only Proper Style, Gothic Architecture in America*. Boston: New York Graphic Society, 1975.

Miller, Amelia F. *Connecticut River Valley Doorways*. Boston: Boston University, 1983.

Montgomery, Charles F. *American Furniture, The Federal Period*. New York: The Viking Press, 1966.

Montgomery, Florence M. *Textiles in America, 1650–1870*. New York: W. W. Norton & Company, 1984.

Naylor, Gillian. *The Arts and Crafts Movement*. Cambridge, Mass.: The MIT Press, 1971.

O'Donnell, Patricia Chapin. "Grisaille Decorated Kasten of New York," *The Magazine Antiques*, May 1980, pp. 1108–11.

Otto, Celia Jackson. *American Furniture of the Nineteenth Century*. New York: The Viking Press, 1965.

Palmer, Brooks. *The Book of American Clocks*. New York: The Macmillan Co., 1967.

St. George, Robert Blair. *The Wrought Covenant, Source Material for the Study of Craftsmen and Community in Southeastern New England, 1620–1700*. Brockton, Mass.: Brockton Art Center/Fuller Memorial, 1979.

Schwartz, Marvin D., Stanek, Edward J., and True, Douglas K. *The Furniture of John Henry Belter and the Rococo Revival*. New York: E. P. Dutton, 1981.

Smith, Robert C. "Final Busts on Eighteenth-Century Philadelphia Furniture," *The Magazine Antiques*, Dec. 1971, pp. 900–05.

Stoneman, Vernon C. *John and Thomas Seymour, Cabinetmakers in Boston, 1794–1816*. Boston: Special Publications, 1959.

Snyder, John J., Jr., ed. *Philadelphia Furniture and Its Makers*. New York: Main Street/Universe Books, 1975.

Thornton, Peter. *Authentic Decor, The Domestic Interior, 1620–1920*. New York: The Viking Press, 1984.

Tracy, Berry B. "For One of the Most Genteel Residences in the City," *The Metropolitan Museum of Art Bulletin* n.s. xxv (Apr. 1967), pp. 283–91.

Trent, Robert, ed. *Pilgrim Century Furniture, An Historical Survey*. New York: Main Street/Universe Books, 1976.

Silver

Avery, C. Louise. *Early American Silver*. New York: The Century Co., 1930.

Buhler, Kathryn C. *American Silver, 1655–1825, in the Museum of Fine Arts, Boston*. Greenwich, Conn.: New York Graphic Society Limited, 1972.

Buhler, Kathryn C., and Hood, Graham. *American Silver, Garvan and Other Collections in the Yale University Art Gallery*. 2 vols. New Haven: Yale University Press, 1970.

Carpenter, Charles H., Jr., and Carpenter, Mary Grace. *Tiffany Silver*. New York: Dodd, Mead & Company, 1978.

Fales, Martha Gandy. *Early American Silver for the Cautious Collector*. New York: Funk & Wagnalls, 1970.

Flynt, Henry N., and Fales, Martha Gandy. *The Heritage Foundation Collection of Silver*. Old Deerfield, Mass.: The Heritage Foundation, 1968.

Hood, Graham. *American Silver, A History of Style, 1650–1900*. New York: Praeger Publishers, 1971.

Safford, Frances Gruber. "Colonial Silver in The American Wing," *The Metropolitan Museum of Art Bulletin* XLI, no. 1 (Summer 1983).

Ward, Barbara McLean, and Ward, Gerald W. R., eds. *Silver in American Life*. New York: The American Federation of Arts, 1979.

Pewter

Laughlin, Ledlie Irwin. *Pewter in America, Its Makers and Their Marks*. Barre, Mass.: Barre Publishers, 1969.

Montgomery, Charles F. *A History of Pewter in America*. New York: E. P. Dutton, 1978.

Jacobs, Carl. *Guide to American Pewter*. New York: The McBride Co., 1957.

Kerfoot, J. B. *American Pewter*. New York: Crown Publishers, 1942.

Ceramics

Barber, Edwin Atlee. *The Pottery and Porcelain of the United States*. Reprint of combined editions. New York: Feingold & Lewis, 1976.

Barrett, Richard Carter. *Bennington Pottery and Porcelain*. New York: Crown Publishers, 1958.

Evans, Paul. *Art Pottery of the United States*. New York: Charles Scribner's Sons, 1974.

Godden, Geoffrey A. *An Illustrated Encyclopedia of British Pottery and Porcelain*. New York: Crown Publishers, 1966.

Howard, David Sanctuary. *New York and the China Trade*. New York: The New-York Historical Society, 1984.

Hume, Ivor Noël. *A Guide to Artifacts of Colonial America*. New York: Alfred A. Knopf, 1970.

———. *Here Lies Virginia*. New York: Alfred A. Knopf, 1963.

Post, Robert C., ed. *1876, A Centennial Exhibition.* Washington, D.C.: Smithsonian Institution Press, 1976.

Quimby, Ian M. G., ed. *Ceramics in America.* Winterthur Conference Report 1972. Charlottesville: The University Press of Virginia, 1972.

Stradling, J. G. "American Ceramics and the Philadelphia Centennial," *The Magazine Antiques,* July 1976, pp. 146–58.

Watkins, Lura Woodside. *Early New England Potters and Their Wares.* Cambridge, Mass.: Harvard University Press, 1950.

Webster, Donald Blake. *Decorated Stoneware Pottery of North America.* Rutland, Vt.: Charles E. Tuttle Co., 1971.

Glass

Feld, Stuart P. "'Nature in Her Most Seductive Aspects': Louis Comfort Tiffany's Favrile Glass," *The Metropolitan Museum of Art Bulletin* n.s. XXI (Nov. 1962), pp. 101–12.

Frelinghuysen, Alice Cooney. "A Masterpiece of the New England Glass Company at The Metropolitan Museum of Art," *Journal of Glass Studies* 25 (1983): 225–30.

Hume, Ivor Noël. "The Search for New Bremen and the Glass of John Frederick Amelung," *The Magazine Antiques,* Mar. 1964, pp. 310–13.

McKearin, George S., and McKearin, Helen. *American Glass.* New York: Crown Publishers, 1948.

———. *Two Hundred Years of American Blown Glass.* New York: Doubleday & Company, 1950.

Wilson, Kenneth M. *New England Glass and Glassmaking.* New York: Thomas Y. Crowell Co., 1972.

Paintings, Prints, Drawings, and Watercolors

Black, Mary, and Lipman, Jean. *American Folk Painting.* New York: Clarkson N. Potter, 1966.

Burke, Doreen Bolger. *American Paintings in The Metropolitan Museum of Art (A Catalogue of Works by Artists Born between 1846 and 1864),* vol. III. New York: The Metropolitan Museum of Art, 1980.

Comstock, Helen. "Spot News in American Historical Prints, 1755–1800," *The Magazine Antiques,* Nov. 1961, pp. 446–49.

Cooper, Helen A., and others. *John Trumbull, The Hand and Spirit of a Painter.* New Haven: Yale University Art Gallery, 1982.

Gardner, Albert TenEyck, and Feld, Stuart P. *American Paintings, A Catalogue of the Collection of The Metropolitan Museum of Art (Painters Born by 1815).* New York: The Metropolitan Museum of Art, 1965.

Goodrich, Laurence B. *Ralph Earl, Recorder for an Era.* n.p.: The State University of New York, 1967.

Groce, George C., and Wallace, David H. *The New-York Historical Society's Dictionary of Artists in America.* New Haven and London: Yale University Press, 1957.

Howat, John K. *The Hudson River and Its Painters.* Reprint. New York: Penguin Books, 1978.

Lipman, Jean. *American Primitive Painting.* New York: Oxford University Press, 1942.

Lipman, Jean, and Winchester, Alice. *The Flowering of American Folk Art, 1776–1876.* New York: The Viking Press, 1974.

The Metropolitan Museum of Art. "American Drawings, Watercolors, and Prints," *The Metropolitan Museum of Art Bulletin* XXXVII, no. 4 (Spring 1980).

The Metropolitan Museum of Art. *American Paintings & Historical Prints from the Middendorf Collection.* New York, 1967.

Peters, Harry T. *Currier & Ives, Printmakers to the American People.* Garden City, N.Y.: Doubleday, Doran & Co., 1942.

Prown, Jules David. *American Painting from Its Beginnings to the Armory Show.* New York: Skira/Rizzoli, 1980.

Quimby, Ian M. G., ed. *American Painting to 1776: A Reappraisal.* Winterthur Conference Report

1971. Charlottesville: The University Press of Virginia, 1971.

Richardson, Edgar P., Hindle, Brooke, and Miller, Lillian B. *Charles Willson Peale and His World.* New York: Harry N. Abrams, 1982.

Richardson, E. P. *A Short History of Painting in America.* New York: Thomas Y. Crowell Co., 1956.

Shadwell, Wendy J. *American Printmaking, The First 150 Years.* Washington, D.C.: Smithsonian Institution Press, 1969.

Smith, Helen Burr. "A Portrait by John Mare Identified: 'Uncle Jeremiah,'" *The Magazine Antiques,* June 1973, pp. 1184–87.

Spassky, Natalie. "Winslow Homer at The Metropolitan Museum of Art," *The Metropolitan Museum of Art Bulletin* XXXIX, no. 4 (Spring 1982).

Index